D1622707

The Biden Deception

THE BIDEN DECEPTION

MODERATE, OPPORTUNIST, OR THE DEMOCRATS' CRYPTO-SOCIALIST?

GEORGE NEUMAYR

REGNERY
PUBLISHING
A Division of Salem Media Group

Regnery® is a registered trademark of Salem Communications Holding Corporation

ISBN: 978-1-68451-131-0
eISBN: 978-1-68451-133-4
Library of Congress Control Number: 2020936160

Published in the United States by
Regnery Publishing
A Division of Salem Media Group
300 New Jersey Ave NW
Washington, DC 20001
www.Regnery.com

Manufactured in the United States of America

10 9 8 7 6 5 4 3 2 1

Books are available in quantity for promotional or premium use. For information on discounts and terms, please visit our website: www.Regnery.com.

Contents

CHAPTER 1

The Myth: Biden Is a Moderate

"I have the most progressive record of anybody running," Joe Biden blurted out in a moment of honesty before he entered the 2020 campaign.[1] He does, as this book will show. But Biden is also known for his habitual blarney. Just as he is capable of bragging about his leftist record, so he is also capable of duping people about his "moderation"— the Big Lie the media has been pushing ever since he defeated Bernie Sanders in the Democratic primaries.

According to the dominant narrative, Biden is a harmless moderate. That's the claim at the heart of the deception that he uses to conceal his dangerous agenda from the public. Biden portrays himself as a figure capable of "unifying" the country and "working across the aisle."[2] Biden feeds the myth that he is a moderate by playing up his bipartisan bona fides. On the campaign trail during the Democratic primaries, he made the preposterous claim that he would consider a Republican as his running mate.[3] The chances of that happening are nil, given the hard-core leftist composition of the Democratic Party. But Biden, ever the phony, said it anyway. Later, as the primaries wore on and Biden needed to appeal to liberal Democrat voters, he promised to name a liberal woman.

"I've made life difficult for myself by putting intellectual consistency and principle above expediency," Biden has said.[4] What a laughable claim. The truth is that "ordinary Joe" long ago abandoned any sensible politics. As the Democratic Party moved to the hard left, so did he. Today he holds loony liberal views that mark him as a far-left Democrat. True, compared to Bernie Sanders, Biden is more moderate in his rhetoric. But relative to the rest of the country, he is a Big Government leftist and crypto-socialist. A Biden presidency would be anything but moderate. It would combine the worst of the Obama years with the new radicalism of the present-day Democratic Party.

This is, after all, a pol who giddily whispered in Barack Obama's ear that a massive government takeover of health care "was a big fucking deal" and pushed a reluctant Obama to embrace gay marriage in 2012.[5] Biden has bragged that he was the "highest-ranking elected U.S. official to support marriage equality."[6] He has declared, "Transgender equality is the civil rights issue of our time."[7]

"Ordinary Joe" has morphed into something more like Hollywood Joe—an opportunistic dilettante who couldn't care less about the ruinous consequences of extreme environmentalism for Rust Belt industries. His climate change plans read like a memo from Al Gore or Michael Moore. The presumptive Democratic nominee is willing to sacrifice countless jobs in the name of the absurd abstraction so trendy among the leftists who dominate his party: "environmental justice." He has endorsed most of the ludicrous Green New Deal, vowed to ban fracking on federal lands, and promised "net-zero emissions" by 2050. And he has vowed that he "will not accept contributions from oil, gas and coal corporations or executives"—as if the companies that provide Americans with our gas and electricity were mafia dons.[8]

Biden's extreme environmentalism would bankrupt the Rust Belt. Yet despite these destructive fantasies, he has the gall to pose as the candidate of the middle class and to claim that he will leave "no workers behind."

The media, eager to fool independents and Republicans, is naturally helping Biden position himself as a less doctrinaire Democrat for the general election. But it's all a con. Blue-collar Joe vanished decades ago. Biden is far more comfortable on *The Ellen DeGeneres Show* than on the streets of Scranton where he grew up. He has given up Amtrak for private jets and, like his lobbyist siblings and grifter son, has cashed in on his name since he left the Obama White House.

Biden has spent much of the 2020 campaign touting his role as a pioneer of fashionable left-wing causes—from demonizing oil companies over "climate change" to presiding at gay nuptials. (He angrily says that he "didn't have to evolve" on LGBTQ issues; his support for them came early.)[9]

During the Democratic primary debates he said that all of the Democratic candidates were equally left-wing and "on the same page." He was right. On issue after issue Biden has adopted the most hard-line liberal stance. He wants to abolish the death penalty, for example, a position that not even Barack Obama or Hillary Clinton took. "Because we cannot ensure we get death penalty cases right every time, Biden will work to pass legislation to eliminate the death penalty at the federal level, and incentivize states to follow the federal government's example. These individuals should instead serve life sentences without probation or parole," says his campaign website.[10]

As for abortions, Biden's absolutism now extends to advocating that all Americans pay for them. He has bragged about his 100 percent rating from the National Abortion Rights Action League. And he has gone completely quiet on law-and-order issues as a form of politically correct penance for his past remarks on the subject.

All of his extreme positions should be thrown in Biden's face during the general election, lest he hoodwink independents and liberal Republicans. All Donald Trump needs to do is quote Biden back to Biden and ask voters in the battleground states: *Is this really what you want? A candidate who will raise your taxes, wipe out your jobs, regulate your industries into extinction, and turn public schools into laboratories for extreme LGBTQ experiments on vulnerable children?*

Biden appears to have convinced himself that he is a gift to America and a moral authority for the world. He informs us that his sheer decency will get the "world to respect America again." This is quite a claim coming from an admitted plagiarist who supports partial-birth abortion and once told China that he "fully understands" its policy of killing children conceived in excess of its eugenic quotas.

Highlighting his essential dishonesty, Biden launched his campaign with an ad based on a Big Lie about Donald Trump—that he had praised white supremacists who were at the Unite the Right rally in Charlottesville.[11] Trump had done nothing of the kind. He had simply noted that there were peaceful people on both sides of the issue of whether to take down or keep up statues of Robert E. Lee. And Biden has kept up this lie, saying that "everything the president says encourages white supremacists," exposing his supposed desire for unity as a sham.[12]

Biden likes to talk about fighting for the "soul of the nation," even as he corrodes his own soul by habitually lying and espousing shamelessly immoral positions.[13] In the culture war, he is on Planned Parenthood's side—in favor of exploiting the weak and encouraging the selfish. Yet this never stops him from trumpeting his moral credentials and playing the Catholic everyman. "I go to Mass and say the rosary," he has said. "Personally for me, faith, it's all about hope and purpose and strength, and for me, my religion is just an enormous sense of solace."[14]

Biden's Catholicism is as fraudulent as every other part of his public image. He treats his faith as a kind of mascot while betraying its most fundamental teachings. On distinctly Catholic issues—from abortion to embryonic stem cell research to gay marriage—his rating is 0 percent. Bishops and priests have said that they will not give him Communion on account of this record.[15]

Like former presidential candidate John Kerry, whose checkered Catholicism cost him the Catholic vote, Biden's phony faith may very well prove more of a liability than an asset. It is just one more reminder that he is an out-of-touch elitist panting after the trends of the moment. Donald Trump won the Catholic vote in important states in 2016 and could win it again, owing to Biden's unfaithful Catholicism.

But some might ask: Wasn't Biden once a moderate? Here and there, it is true, he cast a few reasonable votes over his decades-long career as a U.S. senator. And one can find some quotations in which he sounds like a conservative. Like Teddy Kennedy, Biden was once hesitant about supporting abortion. "I don't like the Supreme Court decision on abortion. I think it went too far. I don't think that a woman has the sole right to say what should happen to her body," he once said.[16] But then, as the party moved to the left on the issue, he sold his soul to its Planned Parenthood wing and never made comments like those again.

And for the most part, even from the beginning of his career, Biden voted as a liberal Democrat. Back in 1995, the American Conservative Union gave him the anemic rating of 13 percent.

And notice how fast Biden has run away from the few good votes from his past. Take, for instance, his pitiful apology for helping to write the 1994 crime bill signed by Bill Clinton. He was once proud of it. "I was one of those guys in 1987 who tried to run on a platform that Clinton basically ran on in 1992. And that is, for a lack of a better phrase, his 'Third Way.' It worked. It's where the American people are. It's where the Democratic Party should have been. . . . One of the things I'm most angry about in the 2000 election, we're now renegotiating as a party what the hell our message should be and who we are, when for me it was settled in 1992," he has said.[17]

But on Martin Luther King Day in 2020, Biden ran away from his vote for that centrist crime bill, saying, "You know I've been in this fight for a long time. It goes not just to voting rights. It goes to the criminal justice system. I haven't always been right. I know we haven't always gotten things right, but I've always tried." Biden appeared to blame his past support for the bill on the systematic racism all white people are supposed to be guilty of: "There's something we have to admit—not you—we, white America, has to admit, there's still a systematic racism and it goes almost unnoticed by so many of us."[18]

Then there is Biden's reversal on the Hyde Amendment, which prohibits taxpayer funding of abortion. In 2020 he told Planned Parenthood that his vote in favor of the amendment was a mistake and that he did not want to support limiting access to abortion in any way. "For many years as a U.S. senator, I have supported the Hyde Amendment as many, many others have because there was sufficient monies and circumstances where women were able to exercise that right [to abortion], women of color, poor women, women were not able to have access. . . . But circumstances have changed. I can't justify leaving millions of women without access to the care they need and their ability to exercise their constitutionally protected right," he has said.[19]

Or how about his embrace of his far-left primary opponents' views on bankruptcy reform and free higher education? At one point in the 2020 campaign, Biden tweeted out, "Across the country, middle and working class families are being squeezed by debt. This is a massive problem, and one that we need all of the best ideas to solve. That's why today, I'm adopting two plans from @BernieSanders and @ewarren to achieve this." After Bernie finally endorsed him, Biden announced that he was going to continue to crib ideas from him by means of joint working groups. "Joe Biden announces that he and Bernie Sanders agreed to establish 6 policy working groups on issues from immigration, to criminal justice reform: 'We're looking forward to turning that work into positive change for the country,'" ABC reported.[20]

All of these reversals and evolutions—actually his rush to the far left of the Democratic Party—contradict the media's mythology of Biden as a moderate. Yet the media still sustain the myth, saying that Biden represents "normalcy." By which they mean a return to the extreme liberalism of the Obama years. Thus Biden's claim that he will restore "decency" to the White House goes unchallenged. (Biden returns the favor, pandering to the press, promising to suspend Trump's "all-out assault" on the media and saying piously, "We must urgently reverse the trend of threats to the media at home and abroad, and once we have reversed it, we must assure that attacks on our free press are never again acceptable in any corner of society, and certainly not in the White House.")[21]

Emboldened by the sympathetic press, Biden says that he will save America from the "vulgar" Donald Trump. Is this the same Joe Biden who called a voter who challenged him "a horse's ass" and told him he was "full of shit"?[22] Is this the same Joe Biden whose pawing of women, including the wife of a defense secretary, became a source of scandal in the Obama White House?[23] Is this the same Joe Biden who said that he didn't want to debate Trump but beat him up? "I wish I were in high school, I could take him behind the gym. That's what I wish," Biden said.[24] That doesn't sound very presidential. But the media gives him a pass.

The media also gives him a pass on his claim that the Obama White House didn't give off a whiff of scandal, even as its scandals continue to erupt, from his son Hunter's corrupt dealings in China and Ukraine to the unmasking of Michael Flynn (it came out in May 2020 that Biden was one of the Obama officials who requested Flynn's unmasking).

Biden oozes "authenticity," the media purrs. That characterization is remarkable given that his first presidential run was blown up by a plagiarism scandal: Biden had lifted the words of British socialist politician Neil Kinnock to describe his own hardscrabble youth in Pennsylvania.[25] Since when has Biden been authentic? He has been fibbing and plagiarizing all of his life. At Syracuse law school, he was nabbed for ripping off a law review article and putting it into one of his papers. He was given an F in the course and rebuked by his professor.[26]

Authenticity? This is the man who said he was arrested when he tried to visit Nelson Mandela in South Africa, a bogus claim he made up as recently as February 2020. (Biden later admitted that he made up the arrested part; he was just temporarily stopped.)[27]

Despite all of this baggage and more, Biden speaks of his run for the presidency in relentlessly moralistic terms. Thankfully, we can expect Trump to puncture Biden's presumption and posturing. We know the media won't. They accept his claim of moral superiority over Trump without question. One might have thought that in this #MeToo age, given Biden's creepy, handsy penchant for sidling up to women, young and old, and whispering in their ears, a feminist talk show host or two would give him a hard time. But they don't. The Oprahs and Ellens treat him with the respect due to an impeccable, wise, and kindly uncle. He is one of the good guys! No need to put his past under a microscope! Never mind the pictures of him cuddling up to female bikers (as male bikers glare at him angrily) and draping himself, Charlie Rose–like, over the wives and children of senators and cabinet officials.[28]

It will be up to Trump and the conservative media to remind Americans of these moments. Biden is moderate in neither his views nor his demeanor. The following pages will demonstrate how far to the left he has gone, and how ill-qualified he is for the presidency.

CHAPTER 2

"The First Thing I Would Do Is Eliminate Trump's Tax Cut"

The contrast between Joe Biden and Bernie Sanders is not as great as is generally believed. Both men are redistributionists at heart, as the 2020 campaign made clear. "Senator Sanders and I may disagree on tactics, but we share a common vision," Biden has said.

After Sanders left the race, Biden paid tribute to his socialist spirit: "I want to commend Bernie for being a powerful voice for a fairer and more just America. It's voices like Bernie's that refuse to allow us to just accept what is—that refuse to accept we can't change what's wrong in our nation—that refuse to accept the health and well-being of our fellow citizens and our planet isn't our responsibility too. Bernie gets a lot of credit for his passionate advocacy for the issues he cares about. But he doesn't get enough credit for being a voice that forces us all to take a hard look in the mirror and ask if we've done enough." (As we have seen, Biden also agreed to form a working group with Sanders to see how they could harmonize their positions.)

Like most Democrats, Joe Biden has been a consistent tax hiker over his career. But in recent years, as the party moved with Bernie Sanders to the radical left, Biden's position on redistributive taxation has hardened.

Tax hiking, he said, would be his immediate goal as president: "[T]he first thing I would do as president is eliminate [President Trump's] tax cut."

Biden made this promise at a forum hosted by the Poor People's Campaign in Washington, D.C. He told the group, "Number one—we have the greatest income inequity in the history of the United States of America since 1902. And the fact of the matter is, there is plenty—plenty!—of money to go around."

Plenty of money to go around. In other words, Biden justifies higher taxes not by the legitimate needs of the federal government but by the need to fix inequality—that is, by the traditional socialist rationale for redistributing wealth.

So the purpose of America's government is wealth redistribution—something that would have come as a surprise to our Founding Fathers. Our federal government was established to serve the people, not rob them. But as the saying goes, pols who rob Peter to pay Paul can always count on the vote of Paul.

Biden's promise to raise taxes wasn't an idle and random one. It is at the center of his economic platform. As Americans for Tax Reform has documented, he has made the promise at least ten times on the campaign trail, with such variations as "The first step is reverse President Trump's tax cuts for the very wealthy and corporations," "[L]ook, the tax cut he passed for multi-millionaires and billionaires, guess what, when I'm president, it's gone. It's gone," and "[F]olks, on day one, on day one I will move Tump's tax cuts, as well for the super wealthy."

Americans for Tax Reform also points out that the first group to feel Biden's tax hike will not be the wealthy. It will be the middle class. Biden's promise to repeal the tax cuts is a promise to raise taxes. According to Americans for Tax Reform, if the tax cuts were repealed:

- A family of four earning the median income of $73,000 would see a $2,000 tax increase
- A single parent (with one child) making $41,000 would see a $1,300 tax increase

- Millions of low- and middle-income households would be stuck paying the Obamacare individual mandate tax
- Utility bills would go up in all fifty states as a direct result of the corporate income tax increase
- Small employers would face a tax increase due to the repeal of the 20 percent deduction for small business income
- The United States would have the highest corporate income tax rate in the developed world
- Taxes would rise in every state and every congressional district
- The death tax would ensnare more families and businesses
- The AMT would snap back to hit millions of households
- Millions of households would see their child tax credit cut in half
- Millions of households would see their standard deduction cut in half, adding to their tax complexity as they are forced to itemize their deductions and deal with the shoebox full of receipts on top of the refrigerator

As noted by the *New York Times*, thanks to the GOP tax cuts, "Most people got a tax cut." The *NYT* also stated, "To a large degree, the gap between perception and reality on the tax cuts appears to flow from a sustained—and misleading—effort by liberal opponents of the law to brand it as a broad middle-class tax increase."

The *Washington Post* also stated, "Most Americans received a tax cut."

More examples of the benefits stemming from the tax cuts are shown in a recent H&R Block report, which states, "overall tax liability is down 24.9 percent on average." In Biden's home state of Delaware, the report found that residents received a 24.8% tax cut.

Biden also lied to the American people when he ran for Vice President in 2008 when he repeatedly said he would not support any form of any tax that imposed even "one single penny" of tax increase on anyone making less than $250,000. Biden shattered that promise upon taking office.[1]

For Biden, there is always "plenty of money to go around," a phrase he seems to have borrowed from his former boss Barack Obama, who famously said to Joe the Plumber, "If you've got a plumbing business, you're gonna be better off if you've got a whole bunch of customers who can afford to hire you, and right now everybody's so pinched that business is bad for everybody, and I think when you spread the wealth around, it's good for everybody."[2]

"Spreading the wealth around" wasn't, in fact, good for everybody. The economy under the Obama-Biden administration floundered for eight years, never even reaching 3 percent growth. It was an administration of tax hikes, stringent regulation, and horrifically wasteful spending.

Biden's rhetoric about the effects of Trump's tax cut is so bogus that even CNN's Jake Tapper said that "it is not true." Tapper noted that Biden was blatantly lying when he said to the Teamsters, "Did you feel [Trump's tax cut]? Did you get anything from it? Of course not, all of it went to folks at the top."[3]

Biden is the traditional tax-and-spend Democrat. Philip Klein of the *Washington Examiner* analyzed Biden's extravagant spending plans and found them anything but moderate: "He has proposed sweeping spending plans to expand Obamacare, pour money into 'green' energy, increase infrastructure, subsidize housing, and pump more money into education." When Klein added it all up, it amounted to $6.015 trillion over a decade: "That's more than the federal government is expected to spend on Medicaid over the next decade."

According to Klein, Biden plans to spend $1.7 trillion on his climate plan, $1.3 trillion on his infrastructure plan (including such boondoggles as electric cars and high-speed rail), $750 billion on his health care plan, $750 billion on education, $750 billion on post–high school education, $640 billion for housing, and $125 billion to combat the opioid epidemic.[4]

Given these prodigal plans, one can see why Biden's first priority is to raise taxes on middle-class Americans. During the coronavirus crisis, he belittled Trump's stimulus packages, saying to the press that they needed to be a "hell of a lot bigger" and that "Milton Friedman isn't running the show anymore."[5]

Vice President Mike Pence has said, "I think the choice that we face in the country today is a choice between freedom and socialism, increasingly. President Trump has been advocating an agenda that's built on the principles of freedom in the marketplaces, lower taxes, less regulation, more access to energy, better, fair trade deals. But increasingly, whether it be Joe Biden, whether it be Bernie Sanders, whether it be Elizabeth Warren and others in their party, they're advocating a socialist agenda of more government, higher taxes and the same tired policies that created the malaise of the last administration where you saw less than 2 percent economic growth."[6]

Indeed, that is the choice, Biden's denials of socialism notwithstanding. He may reject the label of socialism, but he doesn't reject its redistributionist underpinnings.

Tellingly, Paul Waldman, a left-wing writer at the *Washington Post*, swooned over Biden's tax plans. "Joe Biden is more liberal than he looks," Waldman burbled. "The policy plans he has laid out as part of his campaign are much more progressive than most anyone seems to realize. . . . In fact, [his tax plan] is so liberal—in very good ways—that when he was vice president it would have been considered radical, certainly too much for Barack Obama to have signed into law, or in some cases even suggested."[7]

Conservative writers have also been struck by how far to the left of Obama's tax plans Biden's are.

"[Biden] has staked out a tax policy vision that puts him well to the left of former President Barack Obama," wrote Andrew Wilford, a policy analyst at the National Taxpayers Union Foundation, for *USA Today*.

The Penn Wharton Budget Model score of Biden's tax plan shows that it would raise taxes by $2.3–$2.6 trillion over the next ten years. His campaign's estimate is that his tax plan would raise $3.2 trillion. Taxpayers at every income level will be hit by his litany of tax hikes, with at least 93 percent of each income group above the bottom 20 percent seeing a tax increase.[8]

Peter Suderman of *Reason* magazine calls Biden a "classic big-government liberal" who has followed the Democratic Party to the far left. "Biden is a moderate compared to Sanders, but he is notably to the left of previous Democratic standard-bearers. To describe Biden as a moderate without this context is to ignore the specifics of his agenda and the leftward shift in Democratic Party politics it represents," Suderman wrote. Biden

> has proposed $3.4 trillion worth of tax hikes—more than double what former Secretary of State Hillary Clinton proposed when she ran in 2016.
>
> To some extent, this just makes Joe Biden a Democrat in 2020, a successor to President Obama whose approach to policy could be summed up as: "Obama, but more." That alone puts him to the left of previous presidential nominees.[9]

Like most tax-and-spend Democrats, Biden has no concept of limited government. His political philosophy would inevitably mean greatly expanding the federal government. In fact, one of his core campaign promises is that he will expand the size of government and thereby "restore" the faith of Americans in it. He never once considers that it is the bloated character of the federal government that has diminished Americans' faith in it.

Biden promises to undo every economic and regulatory policy Trump has enacted. He routinely lies about Trump's motives (he says Trump, who doesn't even take a presidential salary, is using the federal government to enrich himself), and for all his talk about uniting the country, he routinely plays class warfare. "This country wasn't built by Wall Street bankers and

CEOs and hedge fund managers. It was built by the American middle class," Biden said, striking a divisive tone at the beginning of his campaign.

But it bears repeating that it is members of the American middle class who should fear Biden the most. Biden's massive spending plans will require taxing them, and his plans to restore Obama's job-destroying regulations will cost them jobs.

A vote for Biden is a vote for higher taxes and an anti-business administration, staffed by big government liberals hungry for ever more tax revenue. Trump has joked that Biden is "not going to be running the government," but will be in a "home someplace" while "radical left socialists" run it for him.[10] That is probably not far from the truth. Under a Biden administration, expect the Beto O'Rourkes to come for your guns and the Elizabeth Warrens to come for your money.

CHAPTER 3

"No One Will Be Deported at All for the First 100 Days"

Desperate to impress the hard-core base of the Democratic Party, Joe Biden keeps moving to the left on illegal immigration. Biden has adopted one of the most liberal positions possible on the question. He has even moved to the left of Barack Obama. Biden supports nothing less than turning America into a sanctuary country.

In 2007, he opposed sanctuary cities, notes *The Hill*. But now his campaign says to the press, "Biden believes that the Trump Administration's approach to immigration, including its crackdown on sanctuary cities and especially its repugnant treatment of migrant children, is contrary to our values as a nation."[1]

Tucker Carlson of Fox News has asked, "Is Joe Biden actually moderate? He hugs people. That doesn't mean he is moderate. On immigration, for example, he is not moderate by anybody's definition."[2]

According to Andrew Arthur of the Center for Immigration Studies, "From his rejection of Trump diplomatic initiatives that have slowed the massive influx of migrants from Central America, to his promises to effectively end immigration enforcement in the United States, and to his vow to push for amnesty 'for nearly 11 million undocumented immigrants,' Biden has staked out positions that are not 'center-left.' They are not even 'open borders.' They are 'open America,' a roadmap to a country that punishes DHS employees who are sworn to enforce the law while promising taxpayer funding to immigrants (legal and illegal), as well as a dead-end to any attempt to control immigration to the United States."[3]

During the 2020 campaign, Biden released a plan for immigration titled, "Plan for Securing our Values as a Nation of Immigrants." In it, he touts Obama's failed immigration policies and promises to push even more of them. He endorses Obama's illegal executive orders and says that he would build upon them.

But there is one part of Obama's record that Biden won't defend: the deportations that took place under his administration. Biden has been critical of the deportations, calling them a "mistake."[4] Asked during the 2020 campaign how he would detain illegal immigrants, he replied, "I would not retain them behind bars. . . . Get rid of all the cages, everybody out of prisons." Biden has made a startling campaign promise: "No one will be deported at all for the first 100 days."

To the extent that he has any plan for addressing illegal immigration, it reads like something La Raza could have whipped up. Naturally, amnesty is the organizing principle of his campaign proposal on illegal immigration. Biden says that he wants a "a roadmap to citizenship for the nearly 11 million people who have been living in and strengthening our country for years."

He falsely implies that amnesty is an American tradition: "As president, Biden will commit significant political capital to finally deliver legislative immigration reform to ensure that the U.S. remains open and welcoming to people from every part of the world—and to bring hard-working people who have enriched our communities and our country, in some cases for decades, out of the shadows. This is not just of concern to Latino communities, this touches families of every heritage and background. There are approximately 1.7 million undocumented immigrants from Asia in the U.S., as well as hundreds of thousands from Europe, the Middle East, Africa, and the Caribbean."

And Biden is, of course, opposed to any wall on the border: "Trump has waged an unrelenting assault on our values and our history as a nation of immigrants. It's wrong, and it stops when Joe Biden is elected president. . . . His obsession with building a wall does nothing to address security challenges while costing taxpayers billions of dollars." (Never mind that in 2006 Biden endorsed a physical barrier, as CNN has reported: "Folks, I voted for a fence, I voted, unlike most Democrats—and some of you won't like it—I voted for 700 miles of fence. But, let me tell you, we can build a fence 40 stories high—unless you change the dynamic in Mexico and—and you will not like this, and—punish American employers who knowingly violate the law when, in fact, they hire illegals. Unless you do those two things, all the rest is window dressing.")

And Biden is opposed to Trump's merit-based approach to legal immigration. In contrast, he promises to "[p]reserve preferences for diversity in the current system. Trump has set his sights on abolishing the Diversity Visa lottery. This is a program that brings up to 50,000 immigrants from underrepresented countries to the U.S. each year. He has disparaged the system as a 'horror show' and repeatedly misrepresents how the lottery is administered, while demonizing and insulting with racist overtones those who receive the visas. Diversity preferences are essential to preserving a robust and vibrant immigration system. As president, Biden will reaffirm our core values and preserve the critical role of diversity preferences to ensure immigrants everywhere have the chance to legally become U.S. citizens."

Biden's plan contains no measures to stop illegal immigration. He simply declares it a non-issue: "We know that immigrants and immigrant communities are not a threat to our security, and the government should never use xenophobia or fear tactics to scare voters for political gain. It's irresponsible and un-American. Building a wall from sea-to-shining-sea is not a serious policy solution—it's a waste of money, and it diverts critical resources away from the real threats."

He gives some lip service to stopping criminals from entering the country, but he clearly doesn't consider illegal immigration per se to be a threat. To the extent that he offers any solution, he endorses a pie-in-the-sky "root causes" approach, whereby the United States somehow fixes the countries from which illegal immigrants are coming. His campaign website explains:

> The worst place to deal with irregular migration is at our own border. Rather than working in a cooperative manner with countries in the region to manage the crisis, Trump's erratic, enforcement-only approach is making things worse. The best way to solve this challenge is to address the underlying violence, instability, and lack of opportunity that is compelling people to leave their homes in the Northern Triangle countries of El Salvador, Guatemala, and Honduras in the first place. As Vice President, Biden was the architect of a major program of U.S. assistance to advance reforms in Central America and address the key factors driving migration.
>
> As president, Biden will pursue a comprehensive strategy to strengthen the security and prosperity of Central America in partnership with the people of the region that:
>
> • Addresses the root causes of migration by fostering greater security, economic development, and respect for the rule of law in Central America. The Northern Triangle is riven by violence, plagued by narco-trafficking, and held in fear by criminal organizations wielding military-grade weapons, and it is particularly dangerous for women and children. Biden will propose a four-year, $4 billion package of assistance for the region, with aid linked to governments in the region delivering measurable reductions in gang and gender-based violence, improvements in legal and educational systems, and implementation of anti-corruption measures, among other things. This support will also be supplemented by international donors and regional partners.

- Strengthen regional humanitarian responses. The inability of the Northern Triangle countries to stem the violence and terror in the region has created a regional refugee challenge. Almost every country in the region is receiving refugees and struggling to protect and care for children and families. As a leader in the region, the U.S. has a responsibility to help our neighbors and partners process and support refugees and asylum seekers. This will also help relieve the pressure at our own border.

- Manage migration through refugee resettlement and other legal programs. Whenever possible, we should enable asylum-seekers to make their claim without undertaking the dangerous journey to the U.S. Biden will update the Central American Minors program for certain children seeking to reunify with U.S. relatives, allowing them to apply for entry from their home countries; expand efforts to register and process refugees in the region for resettlement in the U.S. and other countries; and expand opportunities for individuals seeking temporary worker visas or another form of legal status for which they may qualify to be able to come to the U.S.[5]

Should Biden win the presidency, every single measure the Trump administration has used to stem the tide of illegal immigration will be rolled back, and the crisis on America's southern border will flare up yet again. Biden has promised to pay for the health care of illegal immigrants, which will create one more powerful incentive for illegal immigration. Biden even opposed stopping immigration during the coronavirus pandemic. He blasted Trump's temporary ban on immigration with the cheap shot, "Rather than execute a swift and aggressive effort to ramp up testing, Donald Trump is tweeting incendiary rhetoric about immigrants in the hopes that he can distract everyone from the core truth: he's moved too slowly to contain this virus, and we are all paying the price for it."[6]

The misrepresentation of Biden as a moderate on immigration is pushed by the most extreme amnesty advocates, who are so radical that they saw the Obama-Biden administration as oppressive. Biden told one such advocate to "vote for Trump" if he didn't like his generous immigration plans. The misconception is also bolstered by past comments Biden has made on the subject, comments he has now renounced.

According to Andrew Arthur, Biden's plans are deadly serious: "It would be easy to view 'Uncle Joe's' immigration proposals as a sop to Democratic primary voters, but his history in the Obama administration would suggest that he means every word. As his website states, he 'is back and ready to take a hands-on approach to America's problems!' To the large number of Americans who have identified 'immigration' as the 'most important U.S. problem,' Biden's immoderate 'approach' on the issue should give them pause."[7]

Biden has gone so far as to claim that illegal immigrants are "already Americans." They're "just waiting, waiting for a chance to be able to contribute fully."[8] "You know, 11 million people live in the shadows. I believe they're already American citizens," Biden told the U.S. Hispanic Chamber of Commerce. "These people are just waiting, waiting for a chance to contribute fully. And by that standard, 11 million undocumented aliens are already Americans, in my view."

Biden argues that illegal immigration is not a drag on the economy but a boon to it. "If we want a game changer, the single most important thing we can do for our economy and for America's future is pass immigration reform now," he has said. "I've heard for too damn long how this was going to bankrupt us, and Social Security was going to take a nose-dive, and so on. . . . Well guess what? It's a game changer financially for the country."[9]

He thinks all foreign students should be granted citizenship: "We should be stapling a green card to each one of those degrees as they walk across the stage."[10]

Biden caused controversy by saying that ICE officials should be punished for arresting illegal immigrants guilty of drunk driving. "I think Joe Biden has lost his mind," Tom Homan, former acting director of the Immigration and Customs Enforcement (ICE) agency, told Fox News. "He was in Congress for decades. He knows how this works. There is no prerequisite, you commit any crime to be removed from the United States if you're here illegally. That is the way the law is written in statute. If he doesn't like what ICE is doing then he can change the law, but you cannot fire a law enforcement officer to enforcing the law that he took an oath to enforce, a law that was enacted by Congress. It is a ridiculous statement."[11]

Biden has called illegal immigration a "gift."[12] Yes, it is—to the Democratic Party. Illegal immigration is a windfall of new voters for Democrats.

Even some Democrats, such as Jeh Johnson, Obama's director of homeland security, admit that the Democrats have strayed too far "to the left from the American consensus" on illegal immigration.[13]

Biden doesn't care. He is pandering to his party's base, which clamors for open borders and amnesty. He presents Americans' respect for the law as a vice, not a virtue:

> It is a moral failing and a national shame when a father and his baby daughter drown seeking our shores. When children are locked away in overcrowded detention centers and the government seeks to keep them there indefinitely. When our government argues in court against giving those children toothbrushes and soap. When President Trump uses family separation as a weapon against desperate mothers, fathers, and children seeking safety and a better life. When he threatens massive raids that would break up families who have been in this country for years and targets people at sensitive locations like hospitals and schools. When children die while in custody due to lack of adequate care.

Trump has waged an unrelenting assault on our values and our history as a nation of immigrants.

It's wrong, and it stops when Joe Biden is elected president.

Unless your ancestors were native to these shores, or forcibly enslaved and brought here as part of our original sin as a nation, most Americans can trace their family history back to a choice—a choice to leave behind everything that was familiar in search of new opportunities and a new life. Joe Biden understands that is an irrefutable source of our strength. Generations of immigrants have come to this country with little more than the clothes on their backs, the hope in their heart, and a desire to claim their own piece of the American Dream. It's the reason we have constantly been able to renew ourselves, to grow better and stronger as a nation, and to meet new challenges. Immigration is essential to who we are as a nation, our core values, and our aspirations for our future. Under a Biden Administration, we will never turn our backs on who we are or that which makes us uniquely and proudly American. The United States deserves an immigration policy that reflects our highest values as a nation.[14]

Biden has also condemned Trump for instituting a travel ban on countries that are terrorist hotbeds, characterizing it as discrimination against Muslims. On his campaign website Biden demands, "Rescind the un-American travel and refugee bans, also referred to as 'Muslim bans.' The Trump Administration's anti-Muslim bias hurts our economy, betrays our values, and can serve as a powerful terrorist recruiting tool. Prohibiting Muslims from entering the country is morally wrong, and there is no intelligence or evidence that suggests it makes our nation more secure. It is yet another abuse of power by the Trump Administration designed to target primarily black and brown immigrants. Biden will immediately rescind the 'Muslim bans.'"[15]

Trump is not the extremist on immigration. Polls consistently favor his position. The extremist is Biden, for whom securing the border is now an alien concept.

Trump's April 2020 executive order suspending immigration could pose problems for Biden, according to the *Washington Post*: "President Trump's sudden announcement that he would bar immigrants from entering the country could present a challenging proposition for probable Democratic nominee Joe Biden, potentially thrusting him back into a tug of war between a Democratic base firmly opposed to stricter border policies and more-moderate voters willing to consider them, particularly during an economic calamity."[16]

The suggestion of this piece is that Biden, in order to appear reasonable during the coronavirus crisis, would have to buck the voices within his party clamoring for open borders. But it is far too late for that. Biden and every other major figure in the party have agreed that the Democratic Party will be a de facto open-borders party. They are all in favor of health care for illegal immigrants, essentially no deportations, no wall, and emasculating border security.

Trump's order called the Democrats' bluff, showing the American public that the party pretending to be oh so careful about risks during the coronavirus crisis is utterly careless when it comes to immigration. Why should anyone take seriously a party that wants the country shut down but its borders left open?

Biden's bitter response to Trump's suspension of immigration indicates that he is going to maintain the party's reckless stance. Leave it to Biden to favor more rights for foreigners than for American citizens during this crisis. He pooh-poohed the idea of citizens leaving their houses but encouraged foreigners to leave theirs. According to Biden ally and Michigan governor Gretchen Whitmer, it was dangerous to let citizens travel between their own houses, even as her party made it clear that they had no problem with travel between countries.

Biden lacked the backbone and common sense to buck his party during the coronavirus crisis. He remained in pander mode. He was still so worried about impressing AOC and company that he stood in solidarity with illegal immigrants.

Biden's babblings on the subject of immigration exposed the depth of unseriousness the Democrats bring to the issue even at a time of national crisis. It showed that the party of "health," supposedly so worried about scarce resources, is willing to expend resources to accommodate immigration. And it showed that the purportedly middle-class Joe didn't care a whit about protecting middle-class American jobs as America slid into recession.

Biden's tone-deaf politics has Republicans fired up for the general election. "[Biden] effectively called for open borders—no deportations—and has already raised his hand for taxpayer-funded health care for illegals," Scott Jennings, a former political aide in the George W. Bush White House, told *Politico*. "So, at the same time he's called for a ban on fracking, he's opening up America to a flood of illegal immigration. I'm sure this will fly in Pennsylvania and the rest of the upper Midwest. This issue—not to mention the tax increases to pay for abortions—will hurt badly in rural areas and in the big Senate races."[17]

Trump is once again displaying his shrewd instincts, taking measures to strengthen the country while Biden and the Democrats tout policies that place the interests of foreigners before Americans.

CHAPTER 4

"Transgender Equality Is the Civil Rights Issue of Our Time"

I f anyone doubts Joe Biden's leftist credentials, all they need to do is look at his emphasis on transgender rights. "Transgender equality is the civil rights issue of our time," he has said.[1]

Such an outlandish claim would normally hurt a presidential nominee. But Biden has calculated that such avant-garde posturing will help him with the base of the Democratic Party even if it cuts against his image as a moderate in tune with the ordinary concerns of the middle class.

It is hard to believe now, but there was once a time, back in the 1970s, when Biden tried to convince people that he was a social conservative. In a 1974 issue of the *Washingtonian*, he presented himself as conservative on most issues, including moral ones. "When it comes to civil rights and civil liberties, I'm a liberal but that's it. I'm really quite conservative on most other issues," he said. "My wife said I was the most socially conservative man she had ever known. I'm a screaming liberal when it comes to senior citizens because I really think they are getting screwed. I'm a liberal on health care because I believe it is a birth right of every human being—not just some damn privilege to be meted out to a few people. But when it comes to issues like abortion, amnesty, and acid, I'm about as liberal as your grandmother."[2]

These days Biden is in favor of abortion, amnesty, and drugs. And he certainly doesn't sound like a grandmother on the subject of transgenderism. Pandering to the most radical elements of the Democratic Party, he is championing the rights of the "non-binary," the latest trendy term for those who reject their biological sex.

"Transgender and non-binary Americans face significant discrimination when seeking employment. To address these unique challenges, Biden will ensure that workforce and entrepreneurial training programs and resources funded by the U.S. Department of Labor and the Small Business Administration focus on and benefit this community," says his campaign website. "He will also provide incentives for states and local governments to adopt programs that help prepare transgender and non-binary people for the workforce and encourage entrepreneurship."

Biden takes credit for "a leading role in the Obama-Biden Administration's repeal of 'Don't Ask, Don't Tell' to allow gay, lesbian, and bisexual service members to serve the country they love without hiding their sexual orientation." And now he promises to reverse Trump's ban on the "non-binary" in the U.S. military: "In June 2016, the Obama-Biden Administration overturned the ban on transgender individuals serving openly, without hiding their gender identity. But Trump reversed this policy, barring transgender patriots from serving openly. This is discriminatory and detrimental to our national security. Every American who is qualified to serve in our military should be able to do so—regardless of sexual orientation or gender identity and without having to hide who they are. Biden will direct the U.S. Department of Defense to allow transgender service members to serve openly, receive needed medical treatment, and be free from discrimination."

Biden's priorities for the military are as out of whack as his priorities for America's schools. He wants to turn both institutions into social engineering labs. Completely disregarding parental concerns and rights, he encourages youth to come out as "transgender." He promises to force schools to adjust by "[g]uaranteeing transgender students have access to facilities based on their gender identity. On his first day in office, Biden will reinstate the Obama-Biden guidance revoked by the Trump-Pence Administration, which will restore transgender students' access to sports, bathrooms, and locker rooms in accordance with their gender identity. He will direct his Department of Education to vigorously enforce and investigate violations of transgender students' civil rights." Before it suspended operations in 2019, the Biden Foundation had a special program for "Trans Youth."

Biden portrays all of this as thoroughly mainstream. But it is not. It represents the most socially liberal policy ever in American politics, and it will come at a high price in terms of lost religious freedom. In order to execute his LGBTQ agenda, Biden will have to suppress the freedom of Christians and other traditionally religious groups who object to it. Where Trump has protected the religious, Biden plans to persecute them in the name of reproductive and LGBTQ rights. "Religion should not be used as license to discriminate, and as president I will oppose legislation to deny LGBTQ equal treatment in public places," he has said.

Biden is determined to force the entire country and all its institutions to bend to his transgender ideology. "It's about freeing the soul of America from the constraints of bigotry, hate, and fear, and opening people's hearts and minds to what binds us all together," he has said. No, it is about corrupting the soul of America and replacing its Judeo-Christian traditions with a Brave New World experiment sure to backfire.

Miranda Devine of the *New York Post* finds Biden's position on transgender matters stunning. It bodes ill for society, she writes:

> If the leading moderate of the Democratic presidential field is promising to make transgender ideology his human-rights priority, we should understand what that means, for women's sports, for schools, for prisons, for the military, for language.
>
> If there is to be no compromise on transgender rights, then the rights of women and girls will have to be sacrificed.

Does Biden not care, for instance, about the right of biological females to compete in team sports on a level playing field, rather than against transgender athletes with all the natural physiological advantages that come from being born male?

How about the right of girls to preserve their modesty in single-sex locker rooms? Or the right of students not to be confused in sex-ed classes by radical gender theory which disputes the biological reality of two sexes.

Like every other minority, transgender people should be protected from discrimination, as our laws demand. But if you take him at his word, what Biden is advocating is the forceful restructuring of society according to the irrational demands of a subsection of a tiny minority. It's no way to win an election.[3]

The Catholic Church, to which Biden belongs, teaches that transgender ideology is a profound affront to God. Many other religions teach the same. But Biden doesn't care; he disregards that teaching just as he disregards his religion's teaching on gay marriage.

In 2016, he began the practice of officiating at weddings—gay weddings, such was his enthusiasm for that cause. "Proud to marry Brian and Joe at my house. Couldn't be happier, two longtime White House staffers, two great guys," he tweeted.[4]

Biden has also made a special pilgrimage to the Stonewall Inn in New York, where homosexuals held one of their first protests fifty years ago. "Think of the incredible, physical, moral courage it took to stand up and fight back," Biden said during his visit.[5]

Biden considers it a point of pride that he supported gay marriage before anyone else in the Obama White House. "I am absolutely comfortable with the fact that men marrying men, women marrying women and heterosexual men and women marrying one another are entitled to the same exact rights, all the civil rights, all the civil liberties," Biden told

NBC in 2012.[6] His early support for gay marriage angered Obama's advisers, who wanted the vice president to wait until Obama formally changed his position in favor of it. Even Obama betrayed some annoyance, saying that Biden had "got out a little bit over his skis."

Biden apologized to him, and shortly thereafter Obama changed his position in favor of gay marriage. Obama accepted the apology, saying, "Would I have preferred to have done this in my own way? In my own terms without there being a lot of notice to everybody that this is where we were going? Sure. But all's well that ends well."[7]

It doesn't look like it's going to end well for Christians and other religious Americans who hold principled objections to the LGBTQ ethos and don't wish to compromise their religious views. They have good reason to fear a Biden presidency. On his campaign website, he offers a series of promises to the LGBTQ community that, if implemented, would wipe out the last vestiges of religious freedom in this country:

> Donald Trump and Mike Pence have given hate against LGBTQ+ individuals safe harbor and rolled back critical protections for the LGBTQ+ community. By blocking the ability of transgender individuals to openly serve their country, denying LGBTQ+ people access to critical health care, proposing policies allowing federally funded homeless shelters to turn away transgender people and federally funded adoption agencies to reject same-sex couples, and failing to address the epidemic of violence against transgender people—particularly transgender women of color—the Trump-Pence Administration has led a systematic effort to undo the progress President Obama and Vice President Biden made.
>
> Hate and discrimination against LGBTQ+ people started long before Trump and Pence took office. Defeating them will not solve the problem, but it is an essential first step in order to resume our march toward equality.

As President, Biden will stand with the LGBTQ+ community to ensure America finally lives up to the promise on which it was founded: equality for all. He will provide the moral leadership to champion equal rights for all LGBTQ+ people, fight to ensure our laws and institutions protect and enforce their rights, and advance LGBTQ+ equality globally. Biden will:

1. Protect LGBTQ+ people from discrimination.
2. Support LGBTQ+ youth.
3. Protect LGBTQ+ individuals from violence and work to end the epidemic of violence against the transgender community, particularly transgender women of color.
4. Expand access to high-quality health care for LGBTQ+ individuals.
5. Ensure fair treatment of LGBTQ+ individuals in the criminal justice system.
6. Collect data necessary to fully support the LGBTQ+ community.
7. Advance global LGBTQ+ rights and development.[8]

At the center of Biden's plan is passage of the Equality Act, which has been held up in Congress owing to its dire implications for all people of faith: "The Equality Act is the best vehicle for ensuring equal rights under the law for LGBTQ+ Americans, and will guarantee that LGBTQ+ individuals are protected under existing civil rights laws. Biden will make enactment of the Equality Act during his first 100 days as President a top legislative priority. Biden will also direct his Cabinet to ensure immediate and full enforcement of the Equality Act across all federal departments and agencies."[9]

Should the Equality Act be signed into law, it would be open season on religious Americans. The law is so over-the-top that even some pro-gay advocates oppose it. University of Virginia law professor Douglas Laycock, a supporter of gay marriage, told *National Review* that the law would "crush" the religious: "It goes very far to stamp out religious exemptions. It regulates religious non-profits. And then it says that [the Religious Freedom Restoration Act] does not apply to any claim under the Equality Act. This would be the first time Congress has limited the reach of RFRA. This is not a good-faith attempt to reconcile competing interests. It is an attempt by one side to grab all the disputed territory and to crush the other side."[10]

Biden's plan for the LGBTQ community is a blizzard of radical proposals. So extensive are they that they would reach into the internal affairs of other countries. Promoting all things LGBTQ would be a top priority of the Biden State Department:

> As President, Biden will restore the United States' standing as a global leader defending LGBTQ+ rights and development and work closely with our partners and like-minded governments to ensure that violence and discrimination against LGBTQ+ individuals do not go unchecked. Within his first week in office, President Biden will issue a Presidential Memorandum prioritizing his administration's support for LGBTQ+ human rights and development worldwide.
>
> Biden will also:
>
> Ensure that human rights are at the center of our engagement with the world. Biden will significantly bolster the offices at the State Department and USAID dedicated to promoting global LGBTQ+ rights and development. He will appoint senior leaders across the government who will champion global equality, including a point person for LGBTQ+ rights on the National Security Council to drive a cohesive message and strategy across our engagement with individual countries and regions. Biden will immediately appoint a Special Envoy for the Human Rights of LGBTQ+ Persons at the Department of State to coordinate diplomatic efforts and

combat homophobia, transphobia, and stigma globally. He will also appoint a Special Coordinator in charge of international LGBTQ+ programming at USAID.

Advance an inclusive human rights agenda that promotes LGBTQ+ rights by integrating them within a broad human rights agenda. A Biden Administration will advance the inherent human rights of all people, irrespective of who they love or how they identify, rather than siloing off LGBTQ+ human rights as something separate or distinct. It will seek to advance the rights of transgender and intersex people, who face particularly extreme marginalization and bias at home and abroad.

Use the full range of our diplomatic tools and foreign assistance to protect and advance human rights and development, and actively combat violence and discrimination. Biden will lead a coalition of like-minded governments and international organizations to advance protections for LGBTQ+ people, fight for decriminalization of LGBTQ+ identities and relationships, and respond swiftly and meaningfully to threats to LGBTQ+ rights or safety globally. When governments move to restrict LGBTQ+ rights, fail to enforce legal protections in place, or allow or foster a climate of intolerance, the Biden Administration, working with partners, will pursue the most effective strategy to influence that government's behavior, including private diplomacy, public statements, multilateral initiatives at United Nations agencies, and concrete, direct pressure. The Biden Administration will aggressively use pressure tactics, as appropriate, including sanctions (such as Global Magnitsky sanctions and visa bans) to respond to violations of human rights, including LGBTQ+ rights.[11]

Turning the State Department into an LGBTQ activist group that meddles in the affairs of other countries is contrary to the history and traditions of America. Just as America has prized its own religious freedom, so it has respected the religious freedom of countries abroad, particularly those that share America's Judeo-Christian origins.

Biden belongs to an international jet set that seeks to de-Christianize the West and remove its theistic foundations. Barack Obama said that he wanted to "fundamentally transform the United States." His administration's marginalization of Christians represented a huge step in that direction. Should Biden win the presidency, he will seek to complete that project in the name of the New Morality rooted not in the Bible and Ten Commandments but in a nihilistic moral relativism that threatens to destroy the historic and cultural core of America.

CHAPTER 5

"Gun Manufacturers, I'm Going to Take You On and I'm Going to Beat You"

The Texas activist Beto O'Rourke famously said that "hell, yes" he wants to confiscate the guns of Americans.[1] Such a raw comment would normally knock someone out of politics. But not in O'Rourke's case. While many Democrats distanced themselves from O'Rourke's remark, Joe Biden wasn't one of them.

Biden sought out O'Rourke's endorsement and, after he received it at a critical moment before Super Tuesday in the Democratic primaries, gushed that he was going to rely upon O'Rourke to solve the gun problem for him: "I want to make something clear. I'm going to guarantee this is not the last you've seen of this guy. You're going to take care of the gun problem with me. You're going to be the one that leads this effort. I'm counting on you."[2]

Biden sounded ready to name O'Rourke his guns czar. Asked by CNN's Anderson Cooper to respond to Americans who think a Biden administration would come for their guns, Biden replied, "Bingo, you're right if you have an assault weapon."[3]

John Lott, writing for *National Review*, says that O'Rourke leaves the "impression that AR-15s are 'weapons of war,'" but they are not. He continues, "In fact, no self-respecting military in the world would use the 'assault weapons' that he wants to confiscate. AR-15s fire the same sorts of bullets as small-game hunting rifles, and do so with the same velocity and rapidity (one bullet per pull of the trigger). In fact, AR-15s aren't allowed for deer hunting in most states because of the fear that they will wound rather than kill the animals. Such small-caliber rounds may cause the deer to die slowly and painfully."[4]

Biden takes great pride in his record on pushing gun restrictions. He even boasts that he is to the left of Bernie Sanders on the issue. In their debates, Biden chided Sanders for an insufficient commitment to gun control. This occasioned the enormous gaffe he committed in a February 2020 debate when he wildly inflated the number of deaths from guns: "One hundred fifty million people have been killed since 2007, when Bernie voted to exempt the gun manufacturers from liability. More than all the wars, including Vietnam, from that point on. Carnage on our streets. And I want to tell you, if I'm elected, NRA—I'm coming for you and gun manufacturers. I'm going to take you on and I'm going to beat you. I'm the only one who has done it."[5]

Biden says that he has a "plan to end our gun violence epidemic."[6] It's more like a plan to end gun ownership in the United States.

His rhetoric about guns is overwhelmingly negative, as if he is unaware of the thousands of innocent lives they save each year and the thousands of crimes they avert. Biden just keeps on scaremongering. He insists on using inflammatory language to describe popular guns such as the AR-15.

His plan amounts to the death of the Second Amendment by a thousand cuts. Biden is proposing an endless list of new restrictions on guns. Here are some of the major ones, according to his campaign website:

> Hold gun manufacturers accountable. In 2005, then-Senator Biden voted against the Protection of Lawful Commerce in Arms Act, but gun manufacturers successfully lobbied Congress to secure its passage. This law protects

these manufacturers from being held civilly liable for their products—a protection granted to no other industry. Biden will prioritize repealing this protection.

Get weapons of war off our streets. The bans on assault weapons and high-capacity magazines that Biden, along with Senator Feinstein, secured in 1994 reduced the lethality of mass shootings. But, in order to secure the passage of the bans, they had to agree to a 10-year sunset provision and when the time came, the Bush Administration failed to extend them. As president, Biden will:

Ban the manufacture and sale of assault weapons and high-capacity magazines. Federal law prevents hunters from hunting migratory game birds with more than three shells in their shotgun. That means our federal law does more to protect ducks than children. It's wrong. Joe Biden will enact legislation to once again ban assault weapons. This time, the bans will be designed based on lessons learned from the 1994 bans. For example, the ban on assault weapons will be designed to prevent manufacturers from circumventing the law by making minor changes that don't limit the weapon's lethality. While working to pass this legislation, Biden will also use his executive authority to ban the importation of assault weapons.

Regulate possession of existing assault weapons under the National Firearms Act. Currently, the National Firearms Act requires individuals possessing machine-guns, silencers, and short-barreled rifles to undergo a background check and register those weapons with the Bureau of Alcohol, Tobacco, Firearms and Explosives (ATF). Due to these requirements, such weapons are rarely used in crimes. As president, Biden will pursue legislation to regulate possession of existing assault weapons under the National Firearms Act.

Buy back the assault weapons and high-capacity magazines already in our communities. Biden will also institute a program to buy back weapons of war currently on our streets. This will give individuals who now possess assault weapons or high-capacity magazines two options: sell the weapons to the government, or register them under the National Firearms Act.

Reduce stockpiling of weapons. In order to reduce the stockpiling of firearms, Biden supports legislation restricting the number of firearms an individual may purchase per month to one.

Keep guns out of dangerous hands. The federal background check system (the National Instant Criminal Background Check System) is one of the best tools we have to prevent gun violence, but it's only effective when it's used. Biden will enact universal background check legislation and close other loopholes that allow people who should be prohibited from purchasing firearms from making those purchases. Specifically, he will:

- Require background checks for all gun sales. Today, an estimated 1 in 5 firearms are sold or transferred without a background check. Biden will enact universal background check legislation, requiring a background check for all gun sales with very limited exceptions, such as gifts between close family members. This will close the so-called "gun show and online sales loophole" that the Obama-Biden Administration narrowed, but which cannot be fully closed by executive action alone.
- Close other loopholes in the federal background check system. In addition to closing the "boyfriend loophole" highlighted below, Biden will:
- Reinstate the Obama-Biden policy to keep guns out of the hands of certain people unable to manage their affairs for mental reasons, which President Trump reversed. In 2016,

the Obama-Biden Administration finalized a rule to make sure the Social Security Administration (SSA) sends to the background check system records that it holds of individuals who are prohibited from purchasing or possessing firearms because they have been adjudicated by the SSA as unable to manage their affairs for mental reasons. But one of the first actions Donald Trump took as president was to reverse this rule. President Biden will enact legislation to codify this policy.

- Close the "hate crime loophole." Biden will enact legislation prohibiting an individual "who has been convicted of a misdemeanor hate crime, or received an enhanced sentence for a misdemeanor because of hate or bias in its commission" from purchasing or possessing a firearm.

- Close the "Charleston loophole." The Charleston loophole allows people to complete a firearms purchase if their background check is not completed within three business days. Biden supports the proposal in the Enhanced Background Checks Act of 2019, which extends the timeline from three to 10 business days. Biden will also direct the Federal Bureau of Investigation (FBI) to put on his desk within his first 100 days as president a report detailing the cases in which background checks are not completed within 10 business days and steps the federal government can take to reduce or eliminate this occurrence.

- Close the "fugitive from justice" loophole created by the Trump Administration. Because of actions by the Trump Administration, records of almost 500,000 fugitives from justice who are prohibited from purchasing firearms were deleted from the background check system. The Biden Administration will restore these records, and enact legislation to make clear that people facing arrest warrants are prohibited from purchasing or possessing firearms.

- End the online sale of firearms and ammunitions. Biden will enact legislation to prohibit all online sales of firearms, ammunition, kits, and gun parts.[7]

Lawrence Keane of the National Shooting Sports Foundation notes that "Middle Class Joe" displays an antipathy toward a gun manufacturing industry that largely employs and serves the middle class. Writing for *National Review*, Keane says, "The sad part is that Biden chose to attack an industry that has grown 171 percent since 2008 and currently employs more than 312,000 Americans from all walks of life in communities across the nation. He's coming after firearms manufacturers that paid $6.8 billion in total taxes and had a total economic impact of more than $52 billion."[8]

None of this is even remotely moderate. As on other issues, on the gun issue Biden has followed the Democratic Party to the far left. Back at the start of his career, he was hesitant to embrace gun control. As Philip Wegmann of RealClearPolitics points out, Biden "earned favorable grades from the NRA during his first two terms—solid B's in 1978 and 1984. He accepted campaign contributions ahead of his second election from the original manufacturer of the AR-15, Colt Industries. He voted to allow the interstate sale of handguns, successful legislation that the press heralded in 1985 as 'a major victory for gun owners, dealers and the National Rifle Association.'"

But now Biden, unlike other skittish Democratic presidential nominees, proudly runs on gun control, says Wegmann: "This is a far cry from previous Democrats who thought they had to send mixed messages, the enduring image being John Kerry dressed up in camouflage and toting a 12-gauge shotgun as he posed with four dead geese in a carefully choreographed photo op on Ohio farmland two weeks before the 2004 presidential election. The campaign was trying to show that the candidate, who supported gun control, supported hunters. It didn't work."[9]

In other words, the issue became of foremost importance to primary voters, and pols like Biden responded accordingly.

Does anybody really think that Biden would stop at assault weapons? Does anybody think he will put judges who respect the Second Amendment on the Supreme Court? Not a chance.

The heated conversation Biden held with a Detroit auto worker in March 2020 revealed his contempt for gun owners. He told the man who asked him about his confiscatory gun plans that he was "full of shit" and a "horse's ass." The man had accused Biden of "actively trying to end the Second Amendment."[10] He is—along with the rest of the elitists who make up the gun-control wing of the Democratic Party. They preach gun control behind their armed guards.

John Lott, writing for *National Review*, calls 2020 the "gun control election": "Biden was Barack Obama's point person in his push for gun control. That wasn't by accident. In choosing Beto O'Rourke, a person who openly brags about not owning a gun, Biden has made the election debate over whether people should even be able to own guns. Make no mistake about it, your right to defend yourself is at stake in November."[11]

CHAPTER 6

How Biden Will Wreck the Courts

One of the most important questions facing the country in 2020 is: Who will control the judiciary? Donald Trump has kept his promise to name Scalia-like judges to the federal courts. What kind of judges would Joe Biden pick? We don't have to guess. He has already given us two indications: Biden has said that he wants to put "a black female" on the Supreme Court;[1] he has also said that he would like to put Barack Obama on the Court "if he would take it."[2]

"And, by the way, I've said years ago that I'll be satisfied when at least half the court represents the country and are women," he has said.[3]

Beyond those ideas—which demonstrate the extent to which left-wing identity politics rules him—Biden has said that he would appoint only "living" constitutionalists on the court.[4] That is equally troubling, insofar as these living constitutionalists are nothing more than liberal judicial activists who will preserve and expand the most politicized rulings of the high Court.

Biden has said on the campaign trail that his ideal judge is one who finds unstated rights in the Constitution—those "rights," of course, that liberals favor: "I argued and continued to argue, and the bulk of academia agrees with this now, is that if in fact there is a right to privacy in the Constitution—it's not mentioned, it's the Ninth Amendment, there are a number of rights in the Constitution—it's also there are a number of other rights that exist that relate to how you view whether or not all the amendments taken together in the constitutional body actually protects people in their privacy. And so they're the kind of judge—I would look to judges, potential nominees, they would have to acknowledge the fact that there are unenumerated rights that are nonetheless constitutional rights; they're not mentioned by name in the Constitution."[5]

In other words, Biden is looking for judges who will legislate from the bench, enabling the Left to achieve through the courts what it can't accomplish legislatively. Such judges deprive the people of the freedom to govern themselves, invent liberal rights out of thin air, and give judicial sanction to bigger and bigger government. As Thomas Sowell wrote for *National Review*, "For more than a century, believers in bigger government have also been believers in having judges interpret the restraints of the Constitution out of existence. They called this 'a living Constitution.' It has in fact been a dying Constitution, as its restraining provisions have been 'interpreted' to mean less and less so that the federal government can do more and more."[6]

Biden regularly complains about the originalist judges Trump has been appointing to the federal judiciary, as they impede the Left's ideological whims. "Look at how the federal court system is changing," Biden has said. "Four more years of the same kind of appointments, you're going to see a court system that is fundamentally, for two generations, locked in a way that's a death grip that does not make any sense. It's as if Robert Bork would be the chief justice, God rest his soul."[7]

Recall that it was Biden who presided over the Bork hearings as head of the Senate Judiciary Committee. His targeting of Bork for his original-intent judicial philosophy had the effect of turning hearings for Supreme Court nominees ever after into brutal ideological battles. From that point on, conservative nominees were subjected to "Borking."

Biden was so manifestly unfair to Bork—he didn't treat him as a serious judge but dismissed him as part of the "Reagan-Meese" agenda to move the Court to the right—that even the *Washington Post* editorialized against Biden:

> While claiming that Judge Bork will have a full and fair hearing, Senator Joseph Biden this week has pledged to civil rights groups that he will lead the opposition to the confirmation. As the Queen of Hearts said to Alice, "Sentence first—Verdict Afterward."
>
> How can he possibly get a fair hearing from Biden, who has already cast himself in the role of prosecutor instead of a juror in the Judiciary Committee? If there is a strong, serious case to be argued against Judge Bork, why do so many Democrats seem unwilling to make it and afraid to listen to the other side?

Biden opposed Bork not because he lacked the legal credentials to be on the Court but because Bork didn't share his left-wing politics. In his opening statement, Biden said to Bork, "Will we retreat from our tradition of progress or will we move forward, continuing to expand and envelop the rights of individuals in a changing world which is bound to have an impact upon those individuals' sense of who they are and what they can do? . . . In passing on this nomination to the Supreme Court, we must also pass judgment on whether or not your particular philosophy is an appropriate one at this time in history."[8]

Bork tried to point out to Biden that judges aren't supposed to reflect the zeitgeist but to interpret the law according to its original meaning. They are not to legislate from the bench. "If a judge abandons intention as his guide, there is no law available to him, and he begins to legislate a social agenda for the American people. That goes well beyond his legitimate powers. He or she then diminishes liberty instead of enhancing it," Bork said. "The truth is that the judge who looks outside the Constitution always looks inside himself and nowhere else."

But Biden dismissed Bork's originalism and played dirty, portraying the judge as a wild-eyed ideologue who would sanction the breaking down of bedroom doors. In his memoir *Promises to Keep*, Biden pats himself on the back for these tactics. He recalls a conversation he had with a colleague:

> "We should make this about privacy," I said. We'd never even have to bring up abortion. The key was *Griswold*. I suggested to Professor Kurland that it was time to do a little test at the local shopping mall. "I tell you what I'll do," I said. "We'll go up there, and I will ask the first three or four people who walk up, 'Do you think a man and woman in the privacy of their own bedroom have a right to make a decision about whether they have a child, use birth control, or what kind of sex they engage in? What do you think?'"
>
> This was not an exercise in which Professor Kurland wished to engage. Asking people their thoughts about sex at a shopping mall on a hot summer day smacked of a bad television gag to the conservative scholar. But we did it anyway. I think Kurland was relieved that we didn't have to seek anybody out. People who knew me would walk up and say, "Hey, Joe," and I'd ask them if they thought married couples had the right to use contraception. They looked at me like I was crazy. "Of course!" And when I asked why, none of them said the right to privacy. They all said, "The Constitution."[9]

Turning Bork into an enemy of "privacy" was a gross caricature of his jurisprudence. Biden was punishing Bork for not adjusting his jurisprudence to the Left's agenda of cultural change. Never mind that that kind of jurisprudence takes decisions out of the hands of the American people and places them in the hands of a tiny number of judges.

Biden considers his role in beating Bork one of the great moments in his career. What he doesn't mention is that it came on the heels of his campaign-ending plagiarism scandal in 1987 and was used to repair his image with liberals, as even his wife Jill has acknowledged: "He needed to be vindicated. It was about Bork, it was about Bork's politics, but it was also about Joe."[10]

His victory came at the expense of the integrity of the confirmation process and led to weak Republican nominations. Anthony Kennedy and David Souter can thank Joe Biden for their appointments.

"I was an intern for Joe Biden on the Senate Judiciary Committee the summer that Robert Bork's nomination to the Supreme Court was defeated in 1987, and watched Senator Biden turn from an opponent of Bork to a supporter of Kennedy because of Kennedy's belief that Americans have natural rights, like privacy," wrote Jeffrey Rosen for *The Atlantic*. "Biden's support of Kennedy was prescient. Kennedy proved on the Court to be the most significant exponent of a natural-rights jurisprudence of this era, expanding the right to privacy to reaffirm the core of *Roe v. Wade*, which legalized abortion, while extending his broad vision of constitutional liberty to protect marriage equality and to question the health-care mandate of the Affordable Care Act."[11]

In 1991, Biden subjected Clarence Thomas to the same ideological inquisition. Biden demanded to know if Thomas would use the "natural law" in any of his decision-making. Thomas denied that he would. But Biden kept asking him the same question, clearly fishing to see if Thomas opposed abortion rights. Years later, Thomas commented on Biden's baiting: "I have no idea what he was talking about. I understood what he was trying to do. I didn't really appreciate it. Natural law was nothing more than a way of tricking me into talking about abortion."[12]

Nothing is more important to liberal presidents than selecting judges who will uphold *Roe v. Wade*. Biden has vowed not only to select judges committed to retaining it but also to press for Congress to make *Roe v. Wade* "law."

Eddie Scarry of the *Washington Examiner* has written, "Biden's foremost concern in picking a Supreme Court justice or a vice president will not be her job qualifications, but her claim to grievance, oppression, and victimhood. . . . Biden's resurrection is framed as though it's some triumph for the centrists in the party. It's not. He has since proven that he's governed by the same social justice rules as the rest."[13]

Biden would agree with Supreme Court justice Sonia Sotomayor that a "wise Latina woman with the richness of her experiences would more often than not reach a better conclusion than a white male who hasn't lived that life."[14]

Biden would also agree with Obama's infamous "empathy" standard for judges. "We need somebody who's got the heart, the empathy, to recognize what it's like to be a young teenage mom," Obama said in 2008. "The empathy to understand what it's like to be poor, or African American, or gay, or disabled, or old. And that's the criteria by which I'm going to be selecting my judges."[15]

Should Biden win the presidency, the politicization of the courts will accelerate under such flaky standards. We just have to look back to the Obama years to see the impact that judicial activists can have on the courts. A Biden presidency would replicate Obama's record on judges and in all likelihood go beyond it.

In a story entitled "Obama's Judges Leave Imprint on U.S. Law," Reuters reported:

> A Reuters review of rulings by the courts over the last two years shows Obama's appointees to the appeals courts have influenced major legal battles likely to ultimately reach the Supreme Court. . . .
>
> In addition to appointing two Supreme Court justices and dozens of district court judges, Obama appointments now make up 55 of the current 168 appeals court judges, according to the judiciary. Obama's current total of 323 district and appeals court appointments, most of them district court

judges, is similar to the tallies achieved by other recent two-term presidents.[16]

This is what is at stake in 2020. Will the judiciary continue on its originalist course as under Trump or revert to the raw activism of the Obama years?

CHAPTER 7

Bidencare

I f you hate Obamacare, get ready for something worse. Joe Biden has
promised "Bidencare," an even more expensive government takeover
of health care.

At a CNN townhall in February 2020, Biden explained how he
would build upon Obamacare:

> Number one, I would restore all the cuts this president has
> made in the [A]ffordable [C]are [A]ct. Across the board. Num-
> ber one. Number two, I'd add what President Obama and I
> wanted to add, but we had trouble. It took five presidents just
> to get us to the place where we were able to pass the [A]fford-
> able [C]are [A]ct, which is a big deal. We did it without a single
> Republican vote, and I spent a lot of time camped out in the
> House and Senate getting those votes to get it done. What we
> wanted to do is add what they call a public option, and that is
> a Medicare-like option. If in fact you wanted to buy into that
> option or if you didn't have the money, you would be able to
> get it for free. So it's Medicare if you want it.

So I add to the Biden option to Obamacare what we wanted to do in the first place, and I add to that the option of being able to have Medicare if you want it, a Medicare-like proposal. If you can't afford, if you qualify for Medicaid and you don't have it in your state, you're automatically enrolled. There is no waiting for anything.[1]

At The Federalist, Christopher Jacobs calls Biden's plan "socialism lite":

Biden's plan includes many similarities to Sanders'. While both Sanders and Biden want to draw contrasts on health care—Sanders to attack Biden as beholden to corporate interests, and Biden to attack Sanders for wanting to demolish Obamacare—their plans contain far more similarities than differences.

By creating a government-run "public option" like Sanders', the Biden plan would also take away health coverage for millions of Americans. . . . a government-run plan would sabotage private insurance, using access to Treasury dollars and other in-built structural advantages. In 2009, the Lewin Group concluded that a government-run health plan, available to all individuals and paying doctors and hospitals at Medicare rates (i.e., less than private insurance), would lead to 119.1 million individuals losing employer coverage.[2]

As Jacobs writes, the costs of Bidencare will be exorbitant:

Like Sanders', Biden's plan would also increase federal spending, on several levels. First, he would allow individuals living in states that have not expanded Medicaid to join the government-run health plan for free. Note that this proposal lets Medicaid-eligible individuals enroll in the government-run plan only—showing a bias in favor of government-run coverage, as opposed to privately run exchange plans or other types of insurance.

Biden would also expand the Obamacare subsidy regime, in three ways. He would:

1. Reduce the maximum amount individuals would pay in premiums from 9.86% of income to no more than 8.5% of income, with federal subsidies making up the difference.
2. Repeal Obamacare's income cap on subsidies, so that families with incomes of more than four times the poverty level ($103,000 for a family of four in 2019) can qualify for subsidies.
3. To lower deductibles and co-payments, link insurance subsidies to a richer "gold" plan, one that covers 80% of an average enrollee's health costs in a given year, rather than the "silver" plan under current law.

All three of these recommendations come from the liberal Urban Institute's Healthy America plan, issued last year. However, they all come with a big price tag.[3]

Health care expert Sally Pipes predicts that Bidencare would usher in a complete government monopoly on health care through regulations that would bankrupt private plans. At InsideSources Pipes argues, "Biden's health plan would devastate private insurance. Along the way, it would force hospitals to close, drive up premiums, and ultimately lead to a government takeover of health insurance."[4]

If you like your doctor and health care plan, you can keep them, Barack Obama famously said. Incredibly, Biden has repeated that line. Pipes says that is no more true now than when Obama said it. People will flock to the public option, which will cause private care premiums to skyrocket, causing a cascade of negative consequences. She writes, "And the cycle would repeat. Enrollment in the public option would beget higher private insurance premiums, which would lead to yet more enrollment in the public plan. As people with cut-rate public insurance comprise a greater and greater share of hospitals' patient loads, their revenues would deteriorate. Many would struggle to keep their doors open. Eventually, private insurers would disappear from the market. The public option would become Americans' only health insurance option."[5]

And then there are the morally objectionable regulations. On his campaign website, Biden discusses how Bidencare will push "reproductive rights":

> Joe Biden believes that every American–regardless of gender, race, income, sexual orientation, or zip code–should have access to affordable and quality health care. Yet racism, sexism, homophobia, transphobia, and other forms of discrimination permeate our health care system just as in every other part of society. As president, Biden will be a champion for improving access to health care and the health of all by:
>
> • Expanding access to contraception and protect the constitutional right to an abortion. The Affordable Care Act made historic progress by ensuring access to free preventive care, including contraception. The Biden Plan will build on that progress. Vice President Biden supports repealing the Hyde Amendment because health care is a right that should not be dependent on one's zip code or income. And, the public option will cover contraception and a woman's constitutional right to choose. In addition, the Biden Plan will:
> • Reverse the Trump Administration and states' all-out assault on women's right to choose. As president, Biden will work to codify *Roe v. Wade*, and his Justice Department

will do everything in its power to stop the rash of state laws that so blatantly violate the constitutional right to an abortion, such as so-called TRAP laws, parental notification requirements, mandatory waiting periods, and ultrasound requirements.

- Restore federal funding for Planned Parenthood. The Obama-Biden administration fought Republican attacks on funding for Planned Parenthood again and again. As president, Biden will reissue guidance specifying that states cannot refuse Medicaid funding for Planned Parenthood and other providers that refer for abortions or provide related information and reverse the Trump Administration's rule preventing Planned Parenthood and certain other family planning programs from obtaining Title X funds.

- Just as the Obama-Biden Administration did, President Biden will rescind the Mexico City Policy (also referred to as the global gag rule) that President Trump reinstated and expanded. This rule currently bars the U.S. federal government from supporting important global health efforts—including for malaria and HIV/AIDS—in developing countries simply because the organizations providing that aid also offer information on abortion services.[6]

Biden is perfectly willing to violate your religious freedom in order to promote this skewed vision of "health care," in which killing unborn children somehow counts as preserving health.

Bidencare has raised hackles not only on the right but also on the left. Jon Walker of The Intercept says Bidencare would take an already complex law and make it worse: "The record is clear. Even without the partisan obstacles of a nihilistic Republican opposition, Democrats have failed to build on the Affordable Care Act—not from a lack of good intentions, but because of the fatal complexity of the law itself. That same complexity has kept the media from reporting on Democratic failures to build on its own law, which has created the space for Biden to be able to pretend that he'll be able to do so. But ultimately, it's as if the party still hasn't figured out how to get the lights to work in the house, but are confident the answer is an expensive addition."[7]

And how will all of Bidencare's promises be paid for? By raising taxes, Biden says breezily. "Officials with Mr. Biden's campaign said his plan would cost $750 billion over 10 years and would be financed by rolling back the $1.5 trillion tax cut Congress passed last year and doubling the tax rate on capital gains for the wealthiest Americans—those with annual incomes of more than $1 million," reports the *New York Times*.[8]

A future of declining and diminishing care awaits an America that embraces Bidencare.

CHAPTER 8

Biden Will Crush Religious Freedom

A Biden presidency would mean a return to the worst of Obama's policies. Like Obama, Biden is committed to a corrosive secularism that seeks to marginalize the traditionally religious.

The Obama years were devastating for Christians. Biden has signaled that he has every intention of resuming the persecution. His view is that LGBTQ rights and abortion rights justify that persecution.

Biden's campaign website speaks of the limits of "religious freedom":

> Religious freedom is a fundamental American value. But states have inappropriately used broad exemptions to allow businesses, medical providers, social service agencies, state and local government officials, and others to discriminate against LGBTQ+ people. The Trump-Pence Administration has deliberately and systematically attempted to gut protections for the LGBTQ+ community by carving out broad religious exemptions to existing nondiscrimination laws and policies across federal agencies. Biden will reverse Trump's policies misusing

these broad exemptions and fight so that no one is turned away from a business or refused service by a government official just because of who they are or who they love.[1]

Biden would agree with Chai Feldblum, one of Obama's Equal Employment Opportunity commissioners, who holds that the state has an absolute right to violate the religious freedom of Americans who do not support LGBTQ causes. "Just as we do not tolerate private racial beliefs that adversely affect African-Americans in the commercial arena, even if such beliefs are based on religious views, we should similarly not tolerate private beliefs about sexual orientation and gender identity that adversely affect LGBT people," Feldblum said in a 2006 *Brooklyn Law Review* article entitled "Moral Conflict and Liberty: Gay Rights and Religion."

Feldblum called the conflict between the freedom of homosexuals and the freedom of the religious a "zero sum game" in which a "gain for one side necessarily entails a corresponding loss for the other side." The state should see to it that the religious side loses, she wrote.

Religion, she claimed, should have "no relevance" to the state as it referees this game. "Belief liberty," as she puts it, must give way to the "identity liberty" of homosexuals: "Protecting one group's identity may, at times, require that we burden others' belief liberty. This is an inherent and irreconcilable reality of our complex society."

Count on Biden selecting thinkers like Chai Feldblum for his administration. She is a commissar in the Left's campaign to eliminate religion from public life.

The Obama-Biden administration launched one governmental assault on religious freedom after another. The opening salvo came when Obama opined in San Francisco that religion was something that "bitter" Americans cling to in the absence of the consolation of big government. That remark is really just a restatement of Karl Marx's famous line that religion is an "opiate for the masses."

Biden not only favors the Obamacare mandate's forcing the religious to pay for contraceptives and abortifacients for their employees, but he wants to extend it to surgical abortions. He once supported the Hyde Amendment, which prohibited taxpayer funding of abortion, but now loudly and enthusiastically endorses the use of taxpayer money for abortion.

The secularism to which Biden subscribes seeks the death of Christianity by a thousand cuts, some big, some small. Many of those big cuts would come from Biden's judiciary. It is worth recalling some of the secularist radicals that the Obama-Biden administration placed on the courts. They are a preview of the type of jurists Biden would select.

Obama stacked the federal courts with ACLU-style judges who read the First Amendment through an ahistorical and atheistic prism. One of the most egregious is Virginia federal judge Michael Urbanski, who believes that in public settings the Ten Commandments should be reduced to the Six Commandments, the ones that don't mention God. "Could the Ten Commandments be reduced to six, a federal judge asked Monday," reported the *Roanoke Times* in early May 2012.

> That unorthodox suggestion was made by Judge Michael Urbanski during oral arguments over whether the display amounts to a governmental endorsement of religion, as alleged in a lawsuit filed by a student at Narrows High School.
>
> After raising many pointed questions about whether the commandments pass legal muster, the judge referred the case to mediation—with a suggestion: Remove the first four commandments, which are clearly religious in nature, and leave the remaining six, which make more secular commands, such as do not kill or steal.[2]

Another opponent of religious freedom whom Obama elevated to the federal courts is Jesse M. Furman. As a lawyer in private practice, Furman had supported the Anti-Defamation League and other groups in the *Good News Club v. Milford Central School* case, which involved a public elementary school that had blocked an evangelical Christian club for children from using the school facilities for its meetings outside school hours. Furman argued that the school was right to shut the evangelical Christian club out. "While the public school is designed to promote cohesion among a heterogeneous democratic people, the Good News Club is designed to do quite the opposite: to label people as 'saved' or 'unsaved' and, thus, to promote religious belief in general and Christian belief in particular," said Furman. He lost his case before the Supreme Court in a 6–3 opinion.

This is what Joe Biden would call the "living Constitution." He would argue that America has entered into a new and glorious phase in which no one should quibble over such antiquated matters as constitutional limits on the government's powers or the meaning of the First Amendment.

Another chilling prospect is the curtailment of religious freedom that Biden would surely dictate to the U.S. military. Again, the Obama years give us a preview of what to expect from Biden. They were marked by raw intolerance toward Christians. In 2010, Admiral Michael Mullen, chairman of the Joint Chiefs of Staff, gave a briefing to a Special Forces unit at Fort Bragg in North Carolina. During the question-and-answer session, a chaplain opposed to the repeal of "Don't Ask, Don't Tell" asked Mullen whether traditionally Christian chaplains would be "protected" after the ban. Would they be allowed to continue to teach that homosexual acts are morally wrong? No, replied Mullen. "If you cannot get in line, resign your commission," he told the chaplain.

The same message was passed down to privates. As the *Washington Times* reported in 2010, Lieutenant General Thomas P. Bostick, the Army's deputy chief of staff in charge of personnel, told U.S. troops in Germany that soldiers who didn't share Obama's LGBTQ politics should "get out": "Unfortunately, we have a minority of service members who are still racists and bigoted and you will never be able to get rid of all of them. . . . But these people opposing this new policy will need to get with the program, and if they can't, they need to get out."[3]

Under Biden, the conditions for Christian chaplains and privates are sure to get worse. We can expect them to be silenced and court-martialed.

"There is no room for compromise," Biden has said, referring to the collision of religion and the Left's invented "rights."[4]

Under Obama, that meant persecuting the Little Sisters of the Poor. Under Biden, it will mean penalizing churches that do not conform to the New Morality of the Left. Biden's own religion, Catholicism, is sure to be targeted for its stances against abortion and gay marriage. A Biden administration would undoubtedly cut off federal contracts to the Catholic Church for not sanctioning gay adoption and the like.

The only religion that escapes Biden's withering secularism is Islam. Biden never speaks of religious freedom in reference to Christians. But he has spoken of it in reference to Islam.

"To that end, as president, I will take decisive steps to renew our American values by returning transparency to our government. We believe in freedom of religion. That's why I'll end the Muslim ban," he has said, mischaracterizing Trump's travel ban.[5]

The Obama-Biden administration, recall, had a policy of appeasement toward Islam. Even as he waged cultural war on Christians, Obama said repeatedly that he was "not at war with Islam." For Obama, the growth of doctrinal Christianity at home was more troubling than the spread of radical Islam abroad. His culture war with Christians was of far more interest to him than were the battles of Afghanistan. Obama held iftar dinners at the White House and spoke of the Koran with enthusiasm, even as he called St. Paul's Letter to the Romans "obscure."

Obama famously told his NASA administrator, Charles Bolden, to reach out to Islam. Bolden informed a reporter with Al Jazeera that when he took the NASA job, Obama had made it clear to him that "he wanted to find a way to reach out to the Muslim world and engage much more with dominantly Muslim nations to help them feel good about their historic contribution to science."[6]

Obama kept up his Islamophilia even as self-identified Muslim terrorists shot up a military base at Fort Hood, tried to blow up a plane over Detroit on Christmas Day, and attempted to bomb tourists in Times Square. Eric Holder, Obama's attorney general, wouldn't even let his subordinates refer to Islamic terrorism, and John Brennan, Obama's CIA director, praised the concept of jihad, calling it a "legitimate tenet of Islam, meaning to purify oneself or one's community."

Like Obama, Biden sees Christianity, not Islam, as an obstacle to progress. Biden's message to Christians is the same as Obama's: either bring your Christianity into line with my liberalism or there's no place for you in the public square.

CHAPTER 9

Biden's Green New Deal

Anyone who doubts that Biden is no longer a moderate need look no further than the extensive anti-business environmental plans on his campaign website. They go on interminably, exceeding ten thousand words. His plan panders to the far left of the Democratic Party at the expense of America's economy.

It turns out that he plagiarized parts of the plan from left-wing environmental groups. "Plagiarism Charge Hits Biden Climate Change Plan," read a *Politico* headline:

> Former Vice President Joe Biden's campaign came under fire on Tuesday for putting out a $1.7 trillion climate change plan that appeared to copy a handful of passages from previously published documents.
>
> The incident recalled the plagiarism incident that helped drive Biden from the 1988 presidential race, though Biden's campaign team called the latest episode an error that was corrected.

"Several citations, some from sources cited in other parts of the plan, were inadvertently left out of the final version of the 22 page document," a Biden spokesperson said in an email. "As soon as we were made aware of it, we updated to include the proper citations."[1]

Biden's plan was clearly designed to buttress his progressive credentials during the primaries. He felt that he had to pacify supporters of the Green New Deal, proposed by Alexandria Ocasio-Cortez and other radicals in the House of Representatives.

"Biden has been trying to take somewhat of a centrist tack, but he has to appease the core of the base if he's going to win the primary," Jim Manley, an aide to former Senate majority leader Harry M. Reid, told the *Washington Post*. "They've needed to start throwing down some solid policies that will appease the left."

At the center of Biden's campaign plan for the environment is climate change alarmism:

> From coastal towns to rural farms to urban centers, climate change poses an existential threat—not just to our environment, but to our health, our communities, our national security, and our economic well-being. It also damages our communities with storms that wreak havoc on our towns and cities and our homes and schools. It puts our national security at risk by leading to regional instability that will require U.S military-supported relief activities and could make areas more vulnerable to terrorist activities.
>
> Vice President Biden knows there is no greater challenge facing our country and our world. Today, he is outlining a bold plan—a Clean Energy Revolution—to address this grave threat and lead the world in addressing the climate emergency.
>
> Biden believes the Green New Deal is a crucial framework for meeting the climate challenges we face. It powerfully

captures two basic truths, which are at the core of his plan: (1) the United States urgently needs to embrace greater ambition on an epic scale to meet the scope of this challenge, and (2) our environment and our economy are completely and totally connected.[2]

In his quest to combat climate change, he promises to outdo the job-crippling policies of the Obama administration and:

1. Ensure the U.S. achieves a 100% clean energy economy and reaches net-zero emissions no later than 2050. On day one, Biden will sign a series of new executive orders with unprecedented reach that go well beyond the Obama-Biden Administration platform and put us on the right track. And, he will demand that Congress enacts legislation in the first year of his presidency that: 1) establishes an enforcement mechanism that includes milestone targets no later than the end of his first term in 2025, 2) makes a historic investment in clean energy and climate research and innovation, 3) incentivizes the rapid deployment of clean energy innovations across the economy, especially in communities most impacted by climate change.
2. Build a stronger, more resilient nation. On day one, Biden will make smart infrastructure investments to rebuild the nation and to ensure that our buildings, water, transportation, and energy infrastructure can withstand the impacts of climate change. Every dollar spent toward rebuilding our roads, bridges, buildings, the electric grid, and our water infrastructure will be used to prevent, reduce, and withstand a changing climate. As President, Biden will use the convening power of government to boost climate resilience efforts by developing regional climate resilience plans, in partnership with local universities and national

labs, for local access to the most relevant science, data, information, tools, and training.

3. Rally the rest of the world to meet the threat of climate change. Climate change is a global challenge that requires decisive action from every country around the world. Joe Biden knows how to stand with America's allies, stand up to adversaries, and level with any world leader about what must be done. He will not only recommit the United States to the Paris Agreement on climate change—he will go much further than that. He will lead an effort to get every major country to ramp up the ambition of their domestic climate targets. He will make sure those commitments are transparent and enforceable, and stop countries from cheating by using America's economic leverage and power of example. He will fully integrate climate change into our foreign policy and national security strategies, as well as our approach to trade.

4. Stand up to the abuse of power by polluters who disproportionately harm communities of color and low-income communities. Vulnerable communities are disproportionately impacted by the climate emergency and pollution. The Biden Administration will take action against fossil fuel companies and other polluters who put profit over people and knowingly harm our environment and poison our communities' air, land, and water, or conceal information regarding potential environmental and health risks. The Biden plan will ensure that communities across the country from Flint, Michigan to Harlan, Kentucky to the New Hampshire Seacoast have access to clean, safe drinking water. And he'll make sure the development of solutions is an inclusive, community-driven process.[3]

Biden says that these plans will not cost workers their jobs. But of course they will. He has cavalierly told coal miners, "Anybody who can go down 3,000 feet in a mine can sure as hell learn to program as well. . . . Anybody who can throw coal into a furnace can learn how to program, for God's sake!"

But according to *The Hill*, the retraining of coal workers is easier said than done: "Although they are often touted as a solution, retraining programs have a questionable record of success. Some displaced coal workers do transition into other fields or industries, but critics say that the jobs that former coal workers usually find tend to pay only $12 to $15 dollars per hour as opposed to the approximate $75,000 a year salary that coal workers had while working in the mines."[4]

Biden paints a breezy view of a future in which clean energy jobs are plentiful and people drive electric cars:

> There are now one million electric vehicles on the road in the United States. But a key barrier to further deployment of these greenhouse-gas reducing vehicles is the lack of charging stations and coordination across all levels of government. As President, Biden will work with our nation's governors and mayors to support the deployment of more than 500,000 new public charging outlets by the end of 2030. In addition, Biden will restore the full electric vehicle tax credit to incentivize the purchase of these vehicles. He will ensure the tax credit is designed to targeted middle class consumers and, to the greatest extent possible, to prioritize the purchase of vehicles made in America. And, he will work to develop a new fuel economy standard that goes beyond what the Obama-Biden Administration put in place.[5]

And ride trains:

Two centuries ago, the first great railroad expansion drove our industrial revolution. Today, the U.S. is lagging behind Europe and China in rail safety and speed. Biden will develop a plan to ensure that America has the cleanest, safest, and fastest rail system in the world—for both passengers and freight.

With respect to passenger rail: He'll start by putting the Northeast Corridor on higher speeds and shrinking the travel time from D.C. to New York by half—and build in conjunction with it a new, safer Hudson River Tunnel. He will make progress toward the completion of the California High Speed Rail project. He will expand the Northeast Corridor to the fast-growing South. Across the Midwest and the Great West, he will begin the construction of an end-to-end high speed rail system that will connect the coasts, unlocking new, affordable access for every American.[6]

Other features of his plan are equally unsound, such as his concept of "environmental justice":

Everyone is already feeling the effects of climate change. But the impacts—on health, economics, and overall quality of life—are far more acute on communities of color, tribal lands, and low-income communities. "Climate change does not affect everyone equally in the United States," according to Rachel Morello-Frosch, lead author of *The Climate Gap*. "People of color and the poor will be hurt the most—unless elected officials and other policymakers intervene."

We cannot turn a blind eye to the way in which environmental burdens and benefits have been and will continue to be distributed unevenly along racial and socioeconomic lines—not just with respect to climate change, but also pollution of our air, water, and land. The evidence of these disproportionate

harms is clear. According to the Asthma and Allergy Foundation of America, African Americans are almost 3 times more
likely to die from asthma related causes than their white coun-
terparts. And, nearly 1 in 2 of Latinos in the US live in counties
where the air doesn't meet EPA public health standards for
smog according to Green Latinos. And according to the U.S.
Federal Government, 40% of the 567 federally recognized
tribes in U.S. live in Alaska where the rapid pace of rising tem-
peratures and melting sea ice and glaciers threaten the critical
infrastructure and traditional livelihoods in the state. Biden
will reinstate federal protections, rolled back by the Trump
Administration, that were designed to protect communities.
He will make it a priority for all agencies to engage in community-driven approaches to develop solutions for environmental
injustices affecting communities of color, low-income, and
indigenous communities.[7]

How will Biden pay for all of this? By raising taxes, he says:

The Biden plan will make a historic investment in our clean
energy future and environmental justice, paid for by rolling
back the Trump tax incentives that enrich corporations at the
expense of American jobs and the environment. Biden's climate and environmental justice proposal will make a federal
investment of $1.7 trillion over the next ten years, leveraging
additional private sector and state and local investments to
total to more than $5 trillion. President Trump's tax cut led
to trillions in stock buybacks and created new incentives to
shift profits abroad. Joe Biden believes we should instead
invest in a Clean Energy Revolution that creates jobs here at
home.

The Biden plan will be paid for by reversing the excesses
of the Trump tax cuts for corporations, reducing incentives

for tax havens, evasion, and outsourcing, ensuring corporations pay their fair share, closing other loopholes in our tax
code that reward wealth not work, and ending subsidies for
fossil fuels.[8]

Mandy Gunasekara, who worked for Trump's Environmental Protection Agency, calls Biden's plan for the environment "disastrous for
working-class families." In *USA Today*, she says it would raise taxes,
"send energy costs sky high, and kill millions of good-paying jobs." And
for what? The plan is ineffectual. She writes: "The central piece of it,
achieving net zero greenhouse gas emissions by 2050, would have little
effect on the climate. One report from the libertarian Cato Institute
found that such a proposal would prevent warming by 0.137 degrees
Celsius by 2100. In other words, the range of negative impacts alongside
the decimation of the entire coal, oil, and natural gas industries would
all be in exchange for a negligible impact on the climate."[9]

By embracing extreme environmentalism, Biden has made it more
difficult to win the votes of the working class and unions. But he doesn't
seem to care. He has thrown his lot in with the radicals of the party, and
he is committed to sacrificing America's economy on the altar of climate
change ideology.

CHAPTER 10

Biden's Foreign Policy Follies and Corruption

A s a former head of the Senate Foreign Relations Committee, Joe Biden takes great pride in his foreign policy pedigree. He shouldn't. It is a record of failure.

Perhaps nowhere is that clearer than in his criticism of Ronald Reagan at the tail end of the Cold War. While Reagan favored peace through strength, Biden espoused the failed policy of détente. (Biden was a strong supporter of Jimmy Carter. According to Branko Marcetic, author of *Yesterday's Man*, Biden was the first senator to support Carter.)[1]

As the website Discover the Networks chronicles, Biden was wrong about many of Reagan's successful policies:

> Biden was a leading critic of the Reagan defense buildup, specifically vis a vis the MX missile, the B-1 bomber, and the Trident submarine.
>
> Biden criticized President Reagan for his "continued adherence" to the goal of developing a missile defense system known as the Strategic Defense Initiative, calling the

President's insistence on the measure "one of the most reckless and irresponsible acts in the history of modern statecraft."

Biden's opposition to missile defense continued for decades thereafter:

On July 24, 2001 . . . Biden chaired a Senate Foreign Relations Committee hearing in which he said in a prepared statement:

"I worry that funds devoted to missile defense, or the recent tax cut, are hurting our ability to meet these more current and realistic threats. And I worry that a narrow-minded pursuit of missile defense, without having any notion of what missile defense to develop, could derail both our programs in Russia, as well as our negotiations with North Korea."

On July 31, 2007, Biden said:

"In 2001, Bush's new foreign affairs team were so intent on going ahead with Reagan's Star Wars missile defense shield that they were willing to pull out of earlier arms control treaties to get there, inviting, in my view, another arms race. The missile defense system seemed to be the perfect metaphor for the neoisolationist policy. Let's arm the heavens, they were saying, and protect the US, the rest of the world be damned. The [Bush] administration had said they were willing to walk away from the decades-old ABM Treaty in order to unilaterally develop and deploy the missile defense system, and now they were putting real money behind it. They were willing to put tens of billions of dollars into the Maginot line in the sky that could quite likely set off another arms race, while cutting funding for a program to help Russia destroy its nuclear, chemical, and biological weapons before they got into the hands of terrorists."

On December 13, 2007, Biden said:

"[We should] cut somewhere in the order of $20 billion a year out of the military for special programs, from Star Wars, to a new atomic weapon, to the F-22, to the Nimitz-Class Destroyer. You can save $350 billion. That would allow me to do everything I want to do—my priorities on education, health care and the environment—and still bring down the deficit by $150 billion."[2]

Had the conduct of the Cold War been in Biden's hands, it would still be going on.

Biden was also wrong on the Contras in Nicaragua. He opposed funding them. And he was wrong on Iranian policy in the 1970s, as Discover the Networks also notes:

> In 1979 Senator Biden shared President Jimmy Carter's belief that the fall of the Shah in Iran and the advent of Ayatollah Khomeini's rule represented progress for human rights in that country. Throughout the ensuing 444-day hostage crisis, during which Khomeini's extremist acolytes routinely paraded the blindfolded American captives in front of television cameras and threatened them with execution, Biden opposed strong action against the mullahs and called for dialogue.

Joe Biden's stated foreign policy is a collection of platitudes and evidence-free complaints about Donald Trump. Trump promised to keep America out of "stupid wars," and he has. But according to Biden, Trump has somehow destabilized the world. Biden says on his campaign website that to undo Trump's alleged damage to the world, he will hold a "global Summit for Democracy":

> It will bring together the world's democracies to strengthen our democratic institutions, honestly confront nations that are backsliding, and forge a common agenda. Building on the successful model instituted during the Obama-Biden administration with the Nuclear Security Summit, the United States

will prioritize results by galvanizing significant new country commitments in three areas: fighting corruption, defending against authoritarianism, and advancing human rights in their own nations and abroad. As a summit commitment of the United States, I will issue a presidential policy directive that establishes combating corruption as a core national security interest and democratic responsibility, and I will lead efforts internationally to bring transparency to the global financial system, go after illicit tax havens, seize stolen assets, and make it more difficult for leaders who steal from their people to hide behind anonymous front companies.

The Summit for Democracy will also include civil society organizations from around the world that stand on the frontlines in defense of democracy. And the summit members will issue a call to action for the private sector, including technology companies and social media giants, which must recognize their responsibilities and overwhelming interest in preserving democratic societies and protecting free speech. At the same time, free speech cannot serve as a license for technology and social media companies to facilitate the spread of malicious lies. Those companies must act to ensure that their tools and platforms are not empowering the surveillance state, gutting privacy, facilitating repression in China and elsewhere, spreading hate and misinformation, spurring people to violence, or remaining susceptible to other misuse.[3]

He also promises to restore Obama's feckless emphasis on diplomacy to solve world problems:

I am proud of what American diplomacy achieved during the Obama-Biden administration, from driving global efforts to bring the Paris climate agreement into force, to leading the international response to end the Ebola outbreak in West

Africa, to securing the landmark multilateral deal to stop Iran from obtaining nuclear weapons. Diplomacy is not just a series of handshakes and photo ops. It is building and tending relationships and working to identify areas of common interest while managing points of conflict. It requires discipline, a coherent policymaking process, and a team of experienced and empowered professionals. As president, I will elevate diplomacy as the United States' principal tool of foreign policy. I will reinvest in the diplomatic corps, which this administration has hollowed out, and put U.S. diplomacy back in the hands of genuine professionals.[4]

In other words, Biden plans to end Trump's America First policies and put foreign policy in the hands of State Department internationalists willing to sell out American sovereignty.

Biden has bragged that he knows almost all key world leaders and that they have urged him to beat Donald Trump. That might be yet another of his tall tales. But if true, those leaders might want him to replace Trump because Biden is so much easier to manipulate.

Biden has had trouble explaining his foreign policy record on the campaign stump. In Iowa, according to the *Washington Post*, "[O]ne person raised what he called Biden's foreign policy missteps—voting against the 1991 Persian Gulf War, then for the Iraq War; advising Obama against the raid that killed Osama bin Laden—and wondered aloud whether Biden was as sure-footed on foreign policy as he wanted caucusgoers to believe."

On his vote to authorize force in Iraq, Biden has tried to have it both ways, saying that he only supported it to prevent a war from happening. "The threat was to go to war," he has said. "The argument was because Saddam Hussein had weapons of mass destruction, so [President George W. Bush] said that 'I need to be able to get the security council to agree to send in inspectors to put pressure on Saddam to find out whether he's producing nuclear weapons.' At the time, I said, 'that's your reason, alright, I get it.'"

But no one is buying that. Mark Weisbrot of *The Guardian* recalls the important role Biden played in guaranteeing passage of that vote:

> Biden did vastly more than just vote for the war. Yet his role in bringing about that war remains mostly unknown or misunderstood by the public. When the war was debated and then authorized by the US Congress in 2002, Democrats controlled the Senate and Biden was chair of the Senate committee on foreign relations. Biden himself had enormous influence as chair and argued strongly in favor of the 2002 resolution granting President Bush the authority to invade Iraq.
>
> "I do not believe this is a rush to war," Biden said a few days before the vote. "I believe it is a march to peace and security. I believe that failure to overwhelmingly support this resolution is likely to enhance the prospects that war will occur . . ."
>
> But he had a power much greater than his own words. He was able to choose all 18 witnesses in the main Senate hearings on Iraq. And he mainly chose people who supported a pro-war position. They argued in favor of "regime change as the stated US policy" and warned of "a nuclear-armed Saddam sometime in this decade." That Iraqis would "welcome the United States as liberators." And that Iraq "permits known al-Qaida members to live and move freely about in Iraq" and that "they are being supported."

One of the few undeniable successes of the Obama administration was the raid that killed Osama bin Laden. But Biden can't claim any credit for that. In fact, he advised Obama to wait on the raid.

Speaking to House Democrats at a retreat in 2012, he described the discussion about the raid: "The president, he went around the table with all the senior people, including the chiefs of staff, and he said, 'I have to make a decision. What is your opinion?' He started with the national security adviser, the secretary of state, and he ended with me. . . . Every single person in that room hedged their bet except [CIA Director] Leon Panetta. Leon said, 'Go.' . . . He got to me. He said, 'Joe, what do you think?' And I said, 'You know, I didn't know we had so many economists around the table.' I said, 'We owe the man a direct answer. Mr. President, my suggestion is, don't go. We have to do two more things to see if he's there.'"[5]

But Biden being Biden, he has changed this story over the years to make himself look better—an effort for which the *Washington Post*'s fact-checker has given him "Three Pinocchios."

The *New Yorker* noted an "unexpected insult" to Biden in the aftermath of the bin Laden killing: "[D]eclassified documents seized in the raid that killed Osama bin Laden included an unexpected insult: bin Laden had advised assassins to spare Biden and target Obama, telling them, 'Biden is totally unprepared for that post, which will lead the U.S. into a crisis.'"[6]

Biden has taken the view that military spending shouldn't take precedence over domestic spending. In 2014 Biden said, "I saw Vice President Cheney saying that we should be spending more money on our military, not on food stamps and highways. . . . When it comes to the safety of our warriors we have to spend the money. But this idea of it's somehow inherently more important to spend money on the military than on domestic needs is a policy I reject—I reject out of hand."[7]

Donald Trump has made increasing military spending a priority of his administration. We can expect a Biden administration to reject that policy.

Loren Thompson of *Forbes* has written about the changes Americans can expect in foreign policy if the Democrats retake the White House:

> Domestic priorities would eclipse defense spending. Democrats have a more expansive notion of the role of government than Republicans do. Unlike the Trump administration, a Biden or Sanders administration would not try to cut

entitlements or domestic discretionary spending in order to afford a sprawling military establishment. Quite the opposite: given the interests of core Democratic constituencies, they would be more likely to treat military budgets as a bill-payer for domestic initiatives. Thus, the Trump administration's programmed decline of military spending from 3.1% of GDP in 2021 to 2.7% in 2025 would likely unfold faster. . . .

Climate change concerns would rival military strategy. Many Democrats view climate change as the defining strategic challenge of this generation. Military leaders, even those who accept the science surrounding climate change, aren't sure how the problem fits into a national defense framework. Whatever the particulars of a proposed solution might be, it probably won't be good news for military spending plans, or for current operational practices. The Trump administration has largely dismissed "global warming" as a policy issue, but under a President Biden or Sanders, it would rise to the top of national security concerns.

Minorities and women would get more leadership positions. Women and minorities are largely missing from the uppermost tiers of the Trump Pentagon. Aside from the Air Force Secretary and a handful of other players, the ranks of senior political appointees are a very white and very male fraternity. Democrats would definitely change the defense department's leadership demographics to reflect the makeup of the party's base. That's what happened during the Obama years, and it would happen under Biden or Sanders too.

Military veterans are wary of a Biden administration. Veteran John MacDonald, writing for the *Lowell Sun*, summed up how many veterans feel about the possibility of a Biden administration:

From a veteran's perspective the campaign of Joe Biden is almost as bad as nominating Hillary Clinton again. As vice president to the least military and veteran friendly president (President Obama) in recent memory, the sound of Biden for president should send bone-numbing chills through every veteran's body.

Biden was vice president during one of the worst VA scandals in U.S. history. Does anyone remember the waiting lines of death at the VA during the Obama administration?[8]

Biden repeatedly says that Trump has hurt "our allies." But would Israel agree with that? That alliance has never been closer. Should Biden win the presidency, that alliance is sure to weaken as it did during the Obama years. Biden would eliminate all of the Trump policies that have tightened that alliance and bring into his administration many critics of Israel.

"Bob Silverman, a former senior State Department official who served for two-and-a-half years as political counselor at the US Embassy during US president Barack Obama's first term, and now teaches at Jerusalem's Shalem College, said that in order to win the election in November, Biden will be beholden to the Democratic Party's progressive wing. And, he said, 'they are going to insist on a get-tough policy on Israel,' something that might be seen as early as at the Democratic National Convention this summer, when the party's platform is drawn up," reports the *Jerusalem Post*.[9]

And then there is the issue of China. Joe Biden says that he knows better than Trump how to deal with an ascendant China, a remarkable claim given the extent to which Biden has been in the tank for China over the years. Biden helped China get World Trade Organization membership and most-favored-nation trade status. He once dismissed the trade imbalance with China by saying, "It pushes our companies to develop better products and services and our government to craft better policies."[10]

Senator Tom Cotton of Arkansas has gone so far as to say that Biden is "China's choice" for president. Cotton comments in *National Review*:

Despite the occasional box-checking, wishy-washy comment slapping Beijing on the wrist for the worst of its abuses, the reality is that the former vice president's support of the People's Republic of China is deep and longstanding. In the critical fight over whether to grant most-favored-nation trade status and World Trade Organization membership to China in the 1990s—a fight in which, again, many of his party's leaders in Congress were on the right side—Biden carefully shepherded China through the process from his powerful perch as the senior Democrat on the Senate Foreign Relations Committee. Wherever a brake might have been applied—by placing human-rights or labor conditions on most-favored-nation status, for example—Biden voted the measures down and lobbied other senators for Beijing. Unfortunately, China and Biden got their way, and American workers are still suffering from it.[11]

Biden's coziness with China explains why his son Hunter received such a sweetheart deal from the Chinese investment firm BHR Partners. He was reportedly making millions off the firm until media scrutiny forced him to cut ties with it. The Chinese clearly sought to curry favor with Joe Biden through his son: "In 2017, the illustrious vice-presidential son was granted what Chinese commentators described as a Xianchai, a sinecure reserved for offspring of important officials, at BHR Partners. BHR is a $20 billion fund with shareholders that include China Life, China Development Bank and other state-owned entities. China's State Council calls on BHR to find deals abroad by hiring foreigners with political connections," according to Nels Frye in the *New York Post*.[12]

The Trump campaign has taken advantage of Biden's weakness on China. Biden has been nothing if not sunny on the subject of China, as the Trump campaign has eagerly pointed out. The Trump campaign points to such Biden comments as: "Let me be clear: I believed in 1979 and said so then, and I believe now that a rising China is a positive development not only for the people of China but for the United States and the world as a whole"; "You have no safety net. Your policy has been one, which I fully understand and I am not second guessing, of one child per family"; "China is going to eat our lunch? Come on, man. . . . They're not bad folks. . . . They're not competition for us."

Biden has since attempted to hit back, but to no avail. His accusation that Trump has "rolled over for the Chinese" doesn't pass the laugh test. Trump is the first president in years to stand up to China. Even the liberal *New Republic* noted the lameness of a Biden campaign memo attacking Trump's approach to China:

> It is frankly incoherent—the product of an attempt to fit the square peg of preexisting messaging on trade policy into the round hole of "an ongoing catastrophic global pandemic." As one bullet point goes, "Trump entered this election year in need of a deal to stop the bleeding his trade policies had caused, but at the very same time China was misleading the world on the severity of the virus. He was so desperate for a deal that he knowingly let China's mismanagement of the coronavirus pandemic, which has killed tens of thousands of Americans and wrecked our economy, go completely unchallenged."
>
> The memo makes no convincing effort to connect the dots between Trump's tariff negotiations and the administration's coronavirus response, because it is not meant to be an actually coherent argument or narrative; it is meant to be a collection of phrases that resemble arguments but are, in fact, only made up of words voters in focus groups claimed to care about.[13]

The final word on Biden's long record of failure belongs to former defense secretary Robert Gates, who has said of Biden, "I think he's been wrong on nearly every major foreign policy and national security issue over the past four decades."[14]

CHAPTER 11

Biden: Champion of Failing Public Education

In March 2020, the National Education Association (NEA) endorsed Joe Biden for president. The NEA and the very similar American Federation of Teachers are notorious for standing against educational reform in defense of failed public schools. It is no surprise that Biden garnered their endorsement. He has been a consistent defender of the crumbling public education establishment throughout his career.

"I am honored to have the support of the National Education Association—not only America's biggest union, but a preeminent and powerful voice for public school educators and students across the country," Biden said. "I know what it's like to stand shoulder-to-shoulder with a teacher—I've been doing it almost my whole life. That's why I will continue to stand with educators every day on the campaign trail and in the White House. Together, we are going to beat Trump, replace Betsy DeVos, and appoint a Secretary of Education that parents, students, and educators deserve: someone who has worked in a public school classroom."[1]

Biden's education plan consists of throwing more taxpayer money at a broken public school system. His plan contains no attempt to raise standards for public school teachers. Instead, he proposes to give them raises.

His plan would do nothing to improve academic standards for students or give them opportunities outside of the public school system. The plan simply panders to unions like the NEA, which put the interests of bad teachers before students.

Biden's plan completely ignores that the primary problem facing public schools is academic. His education plan is just identity politics by other means. Consider these proposals:

> Invest in our schools to eliminate the funding gap between white and non-white districts, and rich and poor districts. There's an estimated $23 billion annual funding gap between white and non-white school districts today, and gaps persist between high- and low-income districts as well. Biden will work to close this gap by nearly tripling Title I funding, which goes to schools serving a high number of children from low-income families. This new funding will first be used to ensure teachers at Title I schools are paid competitively, three- and four-year olds have access to pre-school, and districts provide access to rigorous coursework across all their schools, not just a few. Once these conditions are met, districts will have the flexibility to use these funds to meet other local priorities. States without a sufficient and equitable finance system will be required to match a share of federal funds.
>
> Improve teacher diversity. Research shows us the substantial and unique impact that teachers of color have on students of color. For example, for black students, having just one black teacher in elementary school reduces the probability of dropping out. Biden will support more innovative approaches to recruiting teachers of color, including supporting high school students in accessing dual-enrollment classes that give them an edge in teacher preparation

programs, helping paraprofessionals work towards their teaching certificate, and working with historically black colleges and universities and other minority-serving institutions to recruit and prepare teachers.

Build the best, most innovative schools in the country in low-income communities and communities of color. Preparing our students for the workforce increasingly entails not only rigorous academics, but also problem-solving, collaboration, and technical skills. Biden will create a new competitive program challenging local communities to reinvent high school to meet these changing demands of work. This funding will be targeted first toward building the best schools in the country in low-income communities and communities of color.

Reinstate the Obama-Biden Administration's actions to diversify our schools. As President, Biden will reinstate Department of Education guidance that supported schools in legally pursuing desegregation strategies and recognized institutions of higher education's interests in creating diverse student bodies. And, he will provide grants to school districts to create plans and implement strategies to diversify their schools.

Make sure children with disabilities have the support to succeed. The Individuals with Disabilities Education Act, signed into law in 1990, promised to provide 40% of the extra cost of special education required by the bill. Currently, the federal government only covers roughly 14% of this cost, failing to live up to our commitment. The Biden Administration will fully fund this obligation within ten years. We must ensure that children with disabilities get the education and training they need to succeed.[2]

America's public schools are failing not because of a lack of money—or of diversity—but because of a lack of standards for teachers and students. But Biden doesn't care about that. He sees education as a means to promote his left-wing racial and gun politics:

> Defeat the National Rifle Association—again—in order to make our schools safer. Parents shouldn't have to worry about whether their kids will come home from school, and students shouldn't have to sacrifice themselves for their friends days before graduation. We cannot let gun violence become an acceptable part of American life. Biden knows that arming teachers isn't the answer; instead, we need rational gun laws. As President, he will secure passage of gun legislation to make our students safer, and he knows he can do it because he's defeated the National Rifle Association twice before. He'll begin by again championing legislation to ban assault weapons and high-capacity magazines—bans he authored in 1994. In the months ahead, he will release additional proposals to address the gun violence epidemic in our country.[3]

Biden's approach to education is hopelessly trendy, as seen in his emphasis not on the need for good teachers but the need for "mental health resources" in public schools:

> Double the number of psychologists, guidance counselors, nurses, social workers, and other health professionals in our schools so our kids get the mental health care they need. One in five children in the U.S. experience mental health problems. Yet, too many of our children are not getting the mental health care they need from a trained professional. We need mental health professionals in our schools to help provide quality mental health care, but we don't have nearly enough. The current school psychologist to student ratio in this country is roughly 1,400 to 1, while experts say it should be at most 700 to 1. That's a gap of about 35,000 to 60,000 school

psychologists. Teachers too often end up having to fill the gap, taking away from their time focusing on teaching. President Biden will make an unprecedented investment in school mental health professionals in order to double the number of psychologists, guidance counselors, nurses, social workers, and other health professionals employed in our schools, and partner with colleges to expand the pipeline of these professionals.[4]

As the press has noted, Biden sent his own children to expensive private schools—even as he opposed private school vouchers for underprivileged children.

"When we divert public funds to private schools, we undermine the entire public education system. We've got to prioritize investing in our public schools, so every kid in America gets a fair shot," he has said. "That's why I oppose vouchers."[5]

Biden opposes all the most hopeful movements in education—from homeschooling to vouchers to charter schools. Of charter schools he has said, "The bottom line is it siphons off money for our public schools, which are already in enough trouble."

Is it any wonder that Randi Weingarten, who heads the American Federation of Teachers, calls Biden "our North Star"?

CHAPTER 12

Biden's Identity Politics

J oe Biden is given to sanctimonious and empty sermonizing about unifying the country. At one of his first campaign rallies for the 2020 Democratic primaries, he said, "I believe America is always better just best when America is acted as one America. One America. One America may be a simple notion, but it doesn't make it any less profound. This nation needs to come together. It has to come together, folks. We started this campaign, and when we did, I said I was running for three reasons. The first is to restore the soul of the nation, the essence of who we are. The second is rebuild the backbone of this nation, and the third to unite this nation. One America."[1]

He has also said, "I believe that we have to end the divisive partisan politics that is ripping this country apart. It's mean-spirited. It's petty. And it's gone on for much too long. I don't believe, like some do, that it's naïve to talk to Republicans. I don't think we should look on Republicans as our enemies."[2]

Even as Biden makes these grand claims, he practices the most cynical racial politics. Recall that he began his campaign with a race-baiting lie: that Trump, after the riot in Charlottesville, Virginia, had called white supremacists "very fine people." That was fake news. But Biden repeated it: "With those words, the president of the United States assigned a moral equivalence between those spreading hate and those with the courage to stand against it."[3] Then he went on TV and continued lying about Trump's record: "He's yet once to condemn white supremacy, the neo-Nazis. He hasn't condemned a darn thing. He has given them oxygen. And that's what's going to continue to happen. That's who this guy is. He has no basic American values—he doesn't understand the American code."[4]

Factcheck.org, a site run by the Annenberg Public Policy Center, rated Biden's claim false:

> Biden's comment that Trump has "yet once to condemn white supremacy" is not accurate.
>
> Let's revisit Trump's comments in the days after the Charlottesville rally. That rally turned violent, and one person, Heather Heyer, was killed and many others injured, when a man with a history of making racist comments plowed his car into a group of counterprotesters.
>
> The day of that incident Trump said, "We condemn in the strongest possible terms this egregious display of hatred, bigotry and violence, on many sides. On many sides." Trump said he had spoken to Virginia Gov. Terry McAuliffe, and "we agreed that the hate and the division must stop, and must stop right now. We have to come together as Americans with love for our nation and true affection—really—and I say this so strongly—true affection for each other."
>
> Two days later, on Aug. 14, 2017, Trump issued a statement from the White House, and referred to "KKK, neo-Nazis, white supremacists, and other hate groups that are repugnant to everything we hold dear as Americans."[5]

During the coronavirus crisis, Biden castigated Trump for "xenophobia," saying his travel bans were racist. Later, when the wisdom of

Trump's bans had become undeniable, he took it back. Biden has a long history of making such charges. Consider his 2012 accusation that the policies of Mitt Romney were going to put blacks "back in chains."[6]

Biden is a shameless practitioner of identity politics who seeks to divide, not unite. And yet he has cast his candidacy as a "return to normalcy." No, it is a return to the divisive and demagogic politics of the Left.

Biden throws around charges of racism wildly, describing anyone who doesn't share his left-wing politics as racist. "The Bull Connors of today don't stand in the street with fire hoses and dogs," he said in a 2020 speech. "They wear nice suits. They wield their power rolling back rights, punishing the poor, denying access to health care and quality education, and turning away refugees and asylum seekers."[7]

In keeping with his identity politics, he has promised to name a woman as his running mate, a move that won him plaudits from the liberal media. The *New Republic* ran a piece entitled "Biden's Diversity Promises Are Identity Politics at Their Best."[8]

He has also said that he would like to make Michelle Obama his running mate. "I'd take her in a heartbeat," Biden told the press in April 2020.[9]

He has promised to place a black woman on the Supreme Court and form a cabinet that "looks like America."[10]

It is clear that diversity, not merit, is the organizing principle of his personnel policy.

Legal scholar Jonathan Turley commented on Biden's toxic identity politics in *The Hill*:

> Biden has taken the position that he will not consider any candidate who is a man or a woman who is white, Asian, Hispanic, or other minority that is not black, no matter how qualified. He would not consider a nominee like Ruth Bader Ginsburg because of the color of her skin. He would not consider Thurgood Marshall because of his gender. Louis

Brandeis and Oliver Wendell Holmes would be losers under this policy.[11]

Biden appears to be following the same course as Walter Mondale, who selected Geraldine Ferraro as his running mate. Mondale's identity politics didn't help him in the slightest.

Biden's identity politics are penance for having supported legislation that liberals deem "anti-black." One can find a few quotations from Biden's senatorial days in which he seems to take the problem of crime seriously: "We must face up to the fact that we don't know how to rehabilitate, that parole boards are not competent, and the certainty of punishment is a deterrent to crime," and "[Americans] are worried about being mugged on the subway. Women are worried about being raped on the way to their automobiles after work. . . . They worry that their government does not seem to be doing much about it, and unfortunately, they appear to be right." These days Biden would never make such comments.

But some hard-core liberals won't let him forget that period of his political career. The title of an Eric Levitz article in *New York* magazine is, "Will Black Voters Still Love Biden When They Remember Who He Was?"

Levitz points out, "Joe Biden once called state-mandated school integration 'the most racist concept you can come up with,' and Barack Obama 'the first sort of mainstream African American who is articulate and bright and clean.' He was a staunch opponent of 'forced busing' in the 1970s, and leading crusader for mass incarceration throughout the '80s and '90s. Uncle Joe has described African-American felons as 'predators' too sociopathic to rehabilitate—and white supremacist senators as his friends."

According to Levitz, "Beyond his role in perpetuating systemic racism (through his opposition to school integration, and support for mass incarceration), Biden has long displayed a penchant for political incorrectness. His suggestion that Barack Obama was the first clean and articulate African-American to run for president is probably the most infamous of his gaffes. But the former vice-president also told a crowd of black voters in 2012 that Mitt Romney would 'put you all back in chains,' and has a habit of badly impersonating Indian convenience-store clerks and call-center employees. But Biden's most troubling 'racially tinged' remarks might be those he does not regard as such. Specifically, the former vice-president has long boasted of his warm—and often legislatively productive—relationships with white supremacist southern senators."[12]

Jamelle Bouie of the *New York Times* is even more brutal in his criticism of Biden, lashing him, given his past record, as the wrong candidate to defeat Trump: "Biden's sensitivity to the fears and anxieties of his white constituents helps explain his positions on drugs and crime in the 1980s and 1990s. He was an ardent drug warrior and 'tough on crime' Democrat who hoped to outflank the Republican Party on those issues, winning ground from worried white voters. 'One of my objectives, quite frankly, is to lock Willie Horton up in jail,' he said in 1990 when he was chairman of the Senate Judiciary Committee."[13]

With criticism like this from the Left, it is no wonder that Biden is busy making affirmative action pledges. He needs to win over liberals skeptical of his past. Biden once said, "I was probably one of those phony liberals. The kind that go out of their way to be nice to a minority. . . ."[14]

Biden is also sensitive to left-wing criticism of his role in the Anita Hill hearings: liberals believe that he was insufficiently protective of her. Biden has tried to put out that fire by saying he would have conducted the hearings differently. But Anita Hill has yet to accept his apology.

"The focus on apology to me is one thing," Anita Hill has said. "But he needs to give an apology to the other women and to the American public because we know now how deeply disappointed Americans around the country were about what they saw. And not just women. There are women and men now who have just really lost confidence in our government to respond to the problem of gender violence."[15]

Biden told the press, of Hill, "I am determined to continue the fight, to see to it that we basically change the culture in this country, where a woman is put in a position that she is disbelieved. . . . She just did not get treated fair across the board. The system did not work."[16]

A pandering Biden as president is a frightening prospect. Anyone who doesn't see how divisive such a presidency would be need only look back at the Obama-Biden administration, which was defined by race-baiting and the deterioration of race relations.

As Pratik Chougule of the *National Interest* commented at the end of Obama's two terms:

> On the causes of and solutions to America's racial divide, black and white views are, to quote a recent Pew finding, "worlds apart." Seventy percent of African-Americans believe that racial discrimination is a major reason why blacks have a harder time getting ahead compared to just 36 percent of white Americans. The groups are divided by a margin of over 40 percentage points on the question of whether blacks are treated less fairly in the workplace and when applying for loans and mortgages. And while 88 percent of African-Americans believe the change is necessary to make equal rights a reality, just over half of white Americans feel the same.
>
> Why, in such a divided country, did Obama choose to inject race, and in such a provocative way?[17]

Recall all the gratuitous and unhelpful comments Obama made about such matters as the Trayvon Martin case ("If I had a son, he'd look like Trayvon") on which he should have remained silent. Biden, as president, would show a similar lack of discipline.

A shallow pol determined to pacify his liberal critics, Biden can also be expected to appease their racial demands, no matter how much they undermine sound policy. Go to Biden's campaign website and almost every section of it is another excuse to bring up more racial grievances. That is a foretaste of a Biden presidency.

The irony is that Biden can't pass his own racial tests. Until he got the nomination, many fellow Democrats considered him a disqualified old white male who should step aside for a minority or female candidate.

After Biden bragged once again about working across the aisle with Republicans, New York City mayor Bill de Blasio tweeted, "It's 2019 & @JoeBiden is longing for the good old days of 'civility' typified by James Eastland. It's past time for apologies or evolution from @JoeBiden. He repeatedly demonstrates that he is out of step with the values of the modern Democratic Party."

Senator Kamala Harris went after Biden for his stance against federally mandated busing, and Cory Booker criticized his participation in the passage of the 1994 crime bill. Unfortunately, getting a dose of his own medicine hasn't made Biden any less willing to play identity politics against Republicans.

Like so many other Democrats, Biden thinks he can beat his opponent by caricaturing the Republican's views as racist. Instead of debating Trump on the merits of immigration policy and other issues, Biden tries to shut down discussion by branding Trump's views as racist.

It is the same sophistical thinking that led Hillary Clinton to tar Trump's supporters as "deplorables." Biden views them with equal disdain. In 2018, Biden called them "virulent" and the "dregs of society." He was speaking before a group of LGBTQ activists, warning that "they—not you—have an ally in the White House. This time they have an ally. They're a small percentage of the American people—virulent people, some of them the dregs of society."[18]

Biden still hasn't learned the lessons of Hillary's defeat: pols who live by identity politics often die by them.

CHAPTER 13

Creepy Joe

Boosters of Joe Biden say that he would restore decorum and dignity to the presidency—a laughable claim on multiple grounds, not the least of which is his mistreatment of women. Though he poses as a feminist, Biden has a long record of treating women improperly.

Liberals have averted their gaze from this problem, but Biden's record is truly off-putting. The incidents range from reports of skinny-dipping in front of female Secret Service agents to the accusation that he assaulted Tara Reade.

In his book *The First Family Detail*, Ronald Kessler reported that "Biden has a habit of swimming in his pool nude. Female Secret Service agents find that offensive." According to Kessler, "Because of Biden's lack of consideration as evidenced by that habit and his refusal to give agents advance notice of his trips back home, being assigned to his detail is considered the second worst assignment in the Secret Service after being assigned to protect Hillary Clinton."[1]

Lucy Flores, who ran for lieutenant governor of Nevada, has written about her experiences with Biden on the campaign trail in a piece for The Cut entitled "An Awkward Kiss Changed How I Saw Joe Biden."

She recounts that at one campaign event he came up behind her, grabbing her back and kissing the back of her head:

> As I was taking deep breaths and preparing myself to make my case to the crowd, I felt two hands on my shoulders. I froze. "Why is the vice-president of the United States touching me?"
>
> I felt him get closer to me from behind. He leaned further in and inhaled my hair. I was mortified. I thought to myself, "I didn't wash my hair today and the vice-president of the United States is smelling it. And also, what in the actual fuck? Why is the vice-president of the United States smelling my hair?" He proceeded to plant a big slow kiss on the back of my head. My brain couldn't process what was happening. I was embarrassed. I was shocked. I was confused. There is a Spanish saying, "tragame tierra," it means, "earth, swallow me whole." I couldn't move and I couldn't say anything. I wanted nothing more than to get Biden away from me. My name was called and I was never happier to get on stage in front of an audience.
>
> I had never experienced anything so blatantly inappropriate and unnerving before. Biden was the second-most powerful man in the country and, arguably, one of the most powerful men in the world. He was there to promote me as the right person for the lieutenant governor job. Instead, he made me feel uneasy, gross, and confused. The vice-president of the United States of America had just touched me in an intimate way reserved for close friends, family, or romantic partners—and I felt powerless to do anything about it.[2]

Numerous other women have suffered the same treatment as Flores. Some of these incidents have been caught on tape. One of the more famous was the time Biden sidled up to Stephanie Carter, the wife of

Defense Secretary Ash Carter, at Carter's swearing-in ceremony and draped himself over her, whispering into her ear.

Several women have complained about Biden touching their necks, rubbing his nose into theirs, and attempting uncomfortable kisses.

In April 2019, Amy Lappos, a Democratic volunteer, came forward to describe her unpleasant encounter with Biden at a fundraiser in Connecticut. "It wasn't sexual, but he did grab me by the head," Amy Lappos said to the *Hartford Courant*. "He put his hand around my neck and pulled me in to rub noses with me. When he was pulling me in, I thought he was going to kiss me on the mouth."[3]

Not even kids are safe from Biden. Recall the moment, caught on tape, when Biden whispered into the ear of the daughter of Senator Chris Coons. The child clearly disliked the treatment and tried to move away from him.

The media has tended to underplay these episodes, casting them as odd but harmless. Mollie Hemingway of The Federalist has noted the double standard in the coverage:

> And if Joe Biden weren't a liberal Democrat? If he were a Republican (particularly one who wasn't liberal and pro-choice—like the recently praised by, uh, Joe Biden Bob Packwood), we'd be talking about how he was engaged in sexual assault against helpless girls and how his micro-aggressions encourage and validate rape culture.
>
> None of us can fully imagine what holy hell would be brought down on a conservative elected official who engaged in behavior like this by more or less everyone in the feminist-media-industrial complex. We wouldn't be seeing jokey headlines. We wouldn't see praise for the White House putting out a video on Biden being Biden. As if.[4]

A handful of feminists have complained about Biden getting a pass. Liza Featherstone of *Jacobin* magazine says that Biden turns his feminism "on and off whenever it's expedient":

When it first became clear that Joe Biden was launching a 2020 campaign for president, a lot of us were amazed that centrist Democrats would, in the #MeToo era, be stupid enough to back his candidacy. But we shouldn't have been surprised: their feminism is fleeting and opportunistic. But the fact that centrist elites were so afraid of social democracy that they did everything they could to advance Biden's candidacy reveals their contempt for women. They're happy to use feminism as a way to temporarily divide and conquer the 99 percent, but if they had any sincere commitment to the advancement of women as a group, they would have lined up behind Bernie Sanders. Failing that, if they were even sincere about advancing female elites, they could have backed one of their many qualified centrist women, who now find themselves in the undignified position of vying to be this clown's vice president.[5]

In March 2020, Tara Reade, a former senate staffer for Biden, made the most serious charge to date against Creepy Joe. She said that he not only kissed and touched her inappropriately but also assaulted her, a charge Biden has denied. As Yahoo News reported:

Reade was a staff assistant for Joe Biden in 1993, when she claims he digitally raped her. She told part of her story in 2019, when Lucy Flores wrote in The Cut about the inappropriate way Biden smelled her hair and kissed the top of her head. At the time, several other women came forward to say that Biden had touched them in ways that made them uncomfortable, including Reade, who said that Biden used to put his hands on her shoulders and run his fingers up and down her neck. Now, she has detailed what she says is the entirety of her experience with Biden on The Katie Halper Show.

According to Reade, Biden pressed her up against a wall and digitally penetrated her [put his finger in her vagina]

without her consent. "It happened all at once, and then . . .
his hands were on me and underneath my clothes," she says.
She also remembers him asking "do you want to go somewhere else?" and then, when she had pulled away, "Come on,
man, I heard you liked me." Reade says that "everything
shattered" in that moment and his claim that he thought she
liked him made her feel like she had "done this" somehow. "I
looked up to him, he was my father's age. He was this champion of women's rights in my eyes," she says. "I wanted to be
a senator; I didn't want to sleep with one."[6]

But not even this allegation has generated any substantial mainstream media coverage. The Media Research Center reported on the
media's silence about the allegation:

Since Reade went public, candidate Biden has given long
interviews, including: an hour-long CNN town hall on March
27, where he faced 23 questions (13 from CNN's Anderson
Cooper, ten others submitted by audience members); nine
minutes on NBC's *Meet the Press* on March 29, where he
faced nine questions from moderator Chuck Todd; and nearly
a quarter-hour on Monday's *MSNBC Live with Katy Tur*,
where he faced an additional nine questions.

   Out of 41 total questions, Biden didn't face a single one
about his new accuser—not exactly the Kavanaugh treatment.
Instead, hosts like NBC's Todd invited Biden to trash his GOP
opponent's response to the coronavirus outbreak: "Do you
think there is blood on the President's hands?"

Even as the Reade accusation received corroboration from members
of her family and friends—and from public records[7]—the media for the
most part continued to ignore her story, in sharp contrast to its treatment
of Supreme Court nominee Brett Kavanaugh. Lynda LaCasse, a neighbor

of Reade's, told Rich McHugh of Business Insider in late April 2020 that Reade had confided in her about the assault:

> LaCasse told Insider that in 1995 or 1996, Reade told her she had been assaulted by Biden. "I remember her saying, here was this person that she was working for and she idolized him," LaCasse said. "And he kind of put her up against a wall. And he put his hand up her skirt and he put his fingers inside her. She felt like she was assaulted, and she really didn't feel there was anything she could do."
>
> LaCasse said that she remembers Reade getting emotional as she told the story. "She was crying," she said. "She was upset. And the more she talked about it, the more she started crying. I remember saying that she needed to file a police report." LaCasse said she does not recall whether Reade supplied any other details, like the location of the alleged assault or anything Biden may have said.
>
> "I don't remember all the details," LaCasse said. "I remember the skirt. I remember the fingers. I remember she was devastated."[8]

Ironically, Biden is on record saying that allegations like these deserve a hearing. He defended Dr. Christine Blasey Ford during the Brett Kavanaugh hearings, saying, "For a woman to come forward in the glaring lights of focus, nationally, you've got to start off with the presumption that at least the essence of what she's talking about is real."[9]

A further irony is that, as vice president, Biden played a role in weakening standards of evidence for sexual assault cases at colleges, as Tucker Carlson pointed out on his Fox News show:

> One of his other jobs was running the administration's Title IX policy. Before the Obama administration, most colleges handled claims of sexual harassment and sexual assault the

way you'd probably want them handled if you were accused of doing something awful. Offenses were narrowly defined as they are in court rather than broadly, and the allegations required had to meet a high burden of proof as they should.

Under Biden's oversight though, the Obama administration changed everything. They sent a letter to every one of the country's more than 4,000 colleges and universities with a stern warning. They said that schools would lose all federal funding unless they completely altered the way they treated sexual assault allegations on campus.

Under the Biden rule, the accused were judged on the lowest standard of evidence. They were subjected to kangaroo courts where they could not effectively use legal counsel or contest the accusations against them. . . .

That was the America that Joe Biden created. What would happen if Joe Biden had to play by the same rules he made now? Well, he'd been [sic] done.[10]

Katie Halper, who helped Reade get her story out, has noted the media's hypocrisy:

Whether you believe Reade or not, it's hard to justify the media's refusal to give her a hearing. When Grim broke Blasey Ford's story, virtually every major US legacy news outlet considered it newsworthy enough to cover within four days. But it took the *New York Times* 19 days to cover Reade's story. The article originally reported that it "found no pattern of sexual misconduct by Mr Biden, beyond the hugs, kisses and touching that women previously said made them uncomfortable." After the publication, the second part of the sentence was deleted at the behest of the Biden campaign, as the paper's executive editor actually admitted: "The campaign thought that the phrasing was awkward and made it look like there were other instances in which he had been accused of sexual misconduct." The *Washington Post*, which took 20 days to report on the story, managed to misquote a police report Reade filed as saying she "disclosed that she believes she was the victim of sexual assault." But the words "she believes" didn't appear in the actual police report.[11]

Like Bill Clinton, Joe Biden seeks absolution for his mistreatment of women by posing as a great champion of women. He takes credit for the Violence Against Women Act of 1994 that helped "establish the first-ever White House Advisor on Violence Against Women during the Obama-Biden Administration," and for helping "launch a national campaign to change the culture surrounding campus rape and sexual assault."

Creepy Joe has a section on his campaign website in which he genuflects before the #MeToo movement:

> In recent years, the #MeToo movement has forced a national reckoning on the depth and breadth of sexual harassment and violence in our workplaces, our campuses, and our communities. Biden has long believed that lasting change starts with addressing the culture and engaging everyone to stand up and speak out against harassment and assault. Building on the success of campaigns targeted at young people, the Biden Administration will launch tools like innovative social awareness campaigns to expand the national movement to end rape culture. It's on all of us to end the violence.
>
> Launch a new friends and family public awareness campaign: Public education about responding to domestic and sexual violence is essential to the well-being of survivors. Research indicates that many survivors disclose abuse to informal sources, namely family members and friends, and positive responses from these disclosures are associated with fewer symptoms of anxiety, depression, and post-traumatic

stress. Biden will launch a new public awareness campaign focusing on what to say and do when someone discloses abuse and how to get that person help. The campaign will also highlight information about evidence-based bystander intervention, including what to do if you witness or become aware of abuse taking place, how to safely intervene, and when to get help.[12]

As for his own victims, Biden is not so sympathetic. He has dismissed the allegations against him as mere misunderstandings: "In my many years on the campaign trail and in public life, I have offered countless handshakes, hugs, expressions of affection, support, and comfort. And not once did I ever believe I acted inappropriately. If it is suggested I did so, I will listen respectfully because it was never my intention."[13]

Like other pawing pols who support abortion rights, Biden counts on feminists to overlook his transgressions out of gratitude for his ideology. One feminist defending Biden even wrote an op-ed in the *New York Times* titled, "I Believe Tara Reade. I Am Voting for Joe Biden Anyway."[14]

Feminists used to call men "male chauvinist pigs." But Biden belongs to a different category: male feminist pigs. He knows that feminists will never attack a Democrat who supports abortion rights. He also knows that if he makes the right pro-feminist noises on issues related to harassment he will be forgiven. "There is no circumstance under which a man has a right to touch a woman without her consent, other than self-defense," Biden has said. "We are changing the attitudes of America about what constitutes appropriate behavior on the part of a man with a woman."[15]

By that standard, Biden is hopelessly guilty. Creepy Joe and presidential dignity don't belong in the same sentence.

CHAPTER 14

Serial Plagiarist

J oe Biden promises to restore "truth" to the White House—a ludicrous claim for a pol who has been exposed as a chronic liar and whose career has been haunted by plagiarism scandals.

Biden's most consequential deception was the plagiarism that forced him to quit the 1988 presidential race. He had plagiarized a speech from a British socialist named Neil Kinnock when speaking at the Iowa State Fair in 1987.

The Kinnock speech read, "Why am I the first Kinnock in a thousand generations to be able to get to university? Was it because our predecessors were thick? Does anybody really think that they didn't get what we had because they didn't have the talent or the strength or the endurance or the commitment? Of course not. It was because there was no platform upon which they could stand."

Biden simply lifted this paragraph and added a few tweaks: "Why is it that Joe Biden is the first in his family ever to go a university? Why is it that my wife . . . is the first in her family to ever go to college? Is it because our fathers and mothers were not bright? . . . Is it because they didn't work hard? My ancestors who worked in the coal mines of northeast Pennsylvania and would come after 12 hours and play football for four hours? It's because they didn't have a platform on which to stand."[1]

This took Biden's copying of socialists to a new level, and it led to a media furor, which in turn led the media to examine other speeches Biden had given. The search turned up the fact that he had also plagiarized from Robert Kennedy and Hubert Humphrey. Biden explained his borrowing from Robert Kennedy by saying, "I thought it was a piece of brilliant work by my staff. . . . I did not know that was an RFK quote. I should have."

Biden was for the most part unrepentant. Maureen Dowd of the *New York Times* reported:

> "I feel real good about that Iowa debate," he said. "I could tell when I was doing my close—that whole audience was absolute dead hushed silence. You can tell when you have it all. And the reason it worked there was, I was the last one. And I decided, I have no close. I didn't have a closing. I'm walking in and they're saying, 'You're going to this debate,' and I said, 'I don't like this stuff you've written for me.'" . . . Advisers to the candidate said that, when it was pointed out to him after the debate that he had followed the Kinnock speech very closely, he was surprised and said he had not been aware of it. They stressed that the Senator had been immersed in difficult preparation for the hearings on Judge Robert H. Bork's nomination to the Supreme Court, an important test for Mr. Biden's political future.
>
> "He was not trying to put something over," said one adviser. "He's under a huge amount of pressure. He didn't even know what he said. He was just on automatic pilot."[2]

As the scandal continued to percolate, the media discovered that Biden had been entangled in a plagiarism scandal at Syracuse law school. As the *Washington Post* reported:

An emotional Sen. Joseph R. Biden Jr. (D-Del.) yesterday acknowledged he had plagiarized in a paper he submitted while a first-year law student in 1965, but defended his integrity and vowed to remain a candidate for his party's presidential nomination.

"I did something very stupid 23 years ago," Biden, chairman of the Senate Judiciary Committee, said at a crowded news conference he convened to try to dispose of burgeoning charges of plagiarism—past and present—that have threatened his candidacy.

He said his 1965 "mistake" was neither intentional nor "malevolent," noted that the faculty of the Syracuse University Law School had allowed him to repeat the course—after initially flunking him for lifting without citation five pages from a published law review, and said that his dean later vouched for his high character. "If anyone tells you Joe Biden isn't a straight arrow, I'd be very surprised," Biden said.[3]

Biden continued to dismiss the significance of his plagiarizing. "In the marketplace of ideas in the political realm, the notion that for every thought or idea you have to go back and find and attribute to someone is frankly ludicrous," the *Washington Post* quoted him as saying.

It also came out during this episode that Biden had poor grades in law school. "Biden said jokingly yesterday that his greatest embarrassment was that his sons were going to find out the mediocrity of his academic record. He said he finished 76th in a class of 86 or 87 at Syracuse, adding, 'I hated law school,'" reported the *Post*.[4]

The 1987 scandal sealed Biden's reputation as a lightweight and a phony. "Just as Mr. [Gary] Hart's relationship with Miss Rice appeared to lend weight to reports that he was a longtime womanizer, so the news that Mr. Biden appropriated whole sections of a law review article and of other politicians' speeches, without giving credit, seemed to many to substantiate assessments that he was shallow and insubstantial—'plastic,' in the lingo of the campaign," wrote R. W. Apple of the *New York Times*.[5]

Did Joe Biden learn his lesson? No, not much has changed since his 1988 presidential run. He continues to lie and plagiarize (his campaign has admitted parts of his environmental plan were lifted from material published by green groups.)

During the 2020 Democratic primaries, Biden got caught out in a huge whopper about getting arrested while trying to visit Nelson Mandela. Politifact rated his claim a "Pants on Fire" lie:

> Here's what Biden said at a Feb. 11 rally in Columbia, S.C.:
>
> "This day, 30 years ago, Nelson Mandela walked out of prison and entered into discussions about apartheid. I had the great honor of meeting him. I had the great honor of being arrested with our U.N. ambassador on the streets of Soweto trying to get to see him on Robbens Island." (It's actually Robben Island.)
>
> The *New York Times* recounted how Biden made similar statements two other times, but reporters could not find evidence to back up his claim that he was arrested. The *Washington Post*'s The Fact Checker then gave Biden Four Pinocchios. Snopes and Factcheck.org also fact-checked his statements.
>
> In the language of PolitiFact, it was a Pants on Fire story. We contacted Biden's campaign to ask about his initial claims that he was arrested, and the later accounts in which he said he was stopped, and did not get a reply.[6]

Biden eventually recanted the story, saying shakily that he had been not arrested but momentarily detained: "When I said 'arrested,' I meant I was not able, I was not able to move, cops, Afrikaners would let me go with them, made me stay where I was. I guess I wasn't arrested, I was stopped. I was not able to move where I wanted to go."

A far more serious whopper Biden has told over the years involves the fatal car accident that killed his first wife and daughter. For years he maintained that the accident was the fault of the truck driver who struck his family: "A tractor-trailer, a guy who allegedly—and I never pursued it—drank his lunch instead of eating his lunch, broadsided my family and killed my wife instantly and killed my daughter instantly and hospitalized my two sons. . . ."

But journalists who looked into the crash found that the truck driver was not drunk and had not violated any traffic rules. The *Newark Post* reported:

> According to Delaware Superior Court Judge Jerome O. Herlihy, who oversaw the police investigation 36 years ago as chief prosecutor, there is no evidence supporting Biden's claim.
>
> "The rumor about alcohol being involved by either party, especially the truck driver (Dunn), is incorrect," Herlihy said recently.
>
> Police determined that Biden's first wife drove into the path of Dunn's tractor-trailer, possibly because her head was turned and she didn't see the oncoming truck.
>
> Dunn, who overturned his rig while swerving to avoid a collision, ran to the wrecked car and was the first to render assistance.
>
> Police filed no charges against Dunn, who at that time lived in North East, Md. with his wife, Ruby, and their seven children.[7]

"We've got to choose truth over lies," Biden has said on the campaign trail. If that's the standard, he has disqualified himself many times over.

CHAPTER 15

Obama's Blundering Veep

Barack Obama's reluctance to endorse Joe Biden for president—he waited until Bernie Sanders exited the race—is surely due in no small part to his memories of Biden's blundering vice presidency, which was full of gaffes, missteps, and ineffectual advice.

Not long into Obama's first term, Biden baffled everyone by saying, "If we do everything right, if we do it with absolute certainty, if we stand up there and we really make the tough decisions, there's still a 30 percent chance we're going to get it wrong."[1]

Get what wrong? Even Obama couldn't decipher Biden's remark, telling the press, "You know, I don't remember exactly what Joe was referring to, not surprisingly."[2]

Biden routinely made such mystifying comments. According to Evan Osnos of the *New Yorker*, Obama aides tried to get the gaffe-prone Biden to rely upon a teleprompter: "At a campaign stop in South Philadelphia, Edward Rendell, the governor of Pennsylvania at the time, was surprised to find workers erecting a teleprompter for Biden. I said, 'Why does Joe have a teleprompter? He never used a teleprompter.' And they said to me, on the Q.T., sort of, "Well, the Obama campaign wants him to be totally scripted, so that he doesn't make any mistakes."[3]

One of Biden's first assignments from Obama was to head up the Middle Class Task Force. But that went nowhere. Biden's idea of helping the middle class was talking up "green jobs" that didn't exist. "We will measure the success or failure of this administration not merely on whether the economy is technically recovered," Biden said, "but on whether the middle class at the end of the day is growing, the middle class is reaping its fair share of growth." On that standard, the Obama administration was a miserable failure.

Biden's Middle Class Task Force, according to *Time*, had no members of the middle class on it:

> [T]he middle class may have a better shot at making ends meet than at influencing the Middle Class Task Force. That's because no member of the Middle Class Task Force is actually middle class. While defining America's most beloved demographic group has never been an exact science, most academics agree that the term refers to anyone earning between $30,000 and $100,000 a year. (Median household income in the U.S. hovers around $50,000.) Every member of the President's task force—from Biden ($227,000) to Council of Economic Advisors Chairwoman Christina Romer ($172,000) to Energy Secretary Steven Chu ($191,000)—makes well over $150,000, putting them in the top 5% of wage earners.
>
> Middle-class Americans are invited to submit questions and ideas through the task force's website, but while tickets for the Philadelphia meeting were distributed to labor and environmental groups, the task force did not accept questions from the audience. "If Biden and his team want to go into this [middle-class issue]," says Daniel Morris, communications director of the Drum Major Institute, a think tank that analyzes middle-class policy issues, "they're going to need to talk

to real members of the middle class. There's no substitute for immediate intimate interaction."[4]

Biden's advice to Obama was typically bad. During the Bush years, Biden had opposed the successful surge in Iraq, and he continued to hold that view under Obama. He told Obama to focus on catching Osama bin Laden, but when the moment came to act, as we have seen, Biden told Obama to wait. To his credit, Obama ignored that advice.

Biden took shots at his predecessor, Dick Cheney, saying that he had created a "divided government" where he had "his own sort of separate national security agency." Biden implied that his conduct as vice president contrasted favorably with Cheney's.

Biden's vice presidency was certainly less consequential than Cheney's. One of the many failed projects of Biden's was overseeing Obama's stimulus package, which manifestly failed to stimulate America's economy.

Biden was sent to various countries to apply Obama's foreign policy, but those efforts proved feckless, as even a few liberals have acknowledged. Andrew Cockburn has written about Biden's Central American forays. Referring to Biden's memoirs, Cockburn said in *Harper's*, "Biden's recollections of his involvement in Central American affairs are no more forthright, and no more insightful. There is no mention of the 2009 coup in Honduras, endorsed and supported by the United States, that displaced the elected president, Manuel Zelaya, nor of that country's subsequent descent into the rule of a corrupt oligarchy accused of ties to drug traffickers. He has nothing but warm words for Juan Orlando Hernández, the current president, who financed his 2013 election campaign with $90 million stolen from the Honduran health service and more recently defied his country's constitution by running for a second term."[5]

Biden was often presented as the Obama administration's expert on foreign policy. Columnist Charles Krauthammer spoke witheringly about Biden's failed foreign policy record:

The Vice President over the last 30 years holds the American record for being wrong on the most issues in Foreign Affairs ever. And the list starts with the nuclear freeze in the early eighties against Thatcher and Reagan, which is one of the follies of the era. . . .

He is the Herbert Hoover of American foreign policy. And for him to be the spokesman for the [Obama] Administration on these affairs, I think is quite ironic.[6]

Like most vice presidents, Biden went to many funerals. He eulogized his close friend Teddy Kennedy, promising that Kennedy's progressive "dream" would live on.

It is humorous to hear Biden say that he would bring dignity back to the White House, given the many times he undermined it as vice president. One of the famous instances was the time he marred Obama's unveiling of Obamacare by whispering loudly in his ear, "This is a big fucking deal!" That intemperate moment led to embarrassing headlines across the country.

Biden's blunders were apparently sufficient to lead Obama's chief of staff to float the possibility of replacing him in 2012. As the *New York Times* reported,

President Obama's top aides secretly considered replacing Vice President Joseph R. Biden Jr. with Hillary Rodham Clinton on the 2012 ticket, undertaking extensive focus-group sessions and polling in late 2011 when Mr. Obama's re-election outlook appeared uncertain.

The aides concluded that despite Mrs. Clinton's popularity, the move would not offer a significant enough political boost to Mr. Obama to justify such a radical move, according to a newly published account of the 2012 race.

The idea of replacing Mr. Biden with Mrs. Clinton had long been rumored, but the journalists Mark Halperin and

John Heilemann, in their new book, "Double Down," provide a detailed description of the effort inside the senior circle of Obama advisers. It was pushed by the chief of staff at the time, William M. Daley, despite the close personal rapport Mr. Daley had developed with Mr. Biden, a fellow Irish Catholic and veteran of Washington politics.

"When the research came back near the end of the year, it suggested that adding Clinton to the ticket wouldn't materially improve Obama's odds," the authors write in their sequel to "Game Change," which chronicled the 2008 campaign. "Biden had dodged a bullet he never saw coming— and never would know anything about, if the Obamans could keep a secret."[7]

In Obama's second term, Biden kept up his gaffes and blunders. His roaming hands got him into as much trouble as his loose lips. Though he was selected to blunt Obama's image as a radical, he ended up playing the role of pushing a leftist agenda. He did so most famously on the issue of gay marriage, endorsing it before Obama did.

In 2016, Obama nominated Merrick Garland to the Supreme Court. But Senate Republicans ignored the nomination, citing "the Biden Rule."[8] As a senator, Biden had said presidents should not nominate anyone to the Supreme Court in an election year:

> Should a justice resign this summer and the president move to name a successor, actions that will occur just days before the Democratic Presidential Convention and weeks before the Republican Convention meets, a process that is already in doubt in the minds of many will become distrusted by all. Senate consideration of a nominee under these circumstances is not fair to the president, to the nominee, or to the Senate itself.
>
> Mr. President, where the nation should be treated to a consideration of constitutional philosophy, all it will get in

such circumstances is a partisan bickering and political posturing from both parties and from both ends of Pennsylvania Avenue. As a result, it is my view that if a Supreme Court Justice resigns tomorrow, or within the next several weeks, or resigns at the end of the summer, President Bush should consider following the practice of a majority of his predecessors and not—and not—name a nominee until after the November election is completed.

Ironically, Biden as a candidate now stands to Obama's left, something even Obama acknowledges. Biden is running on the "most progressive platform ever," Obama has said.

In 2020, all the candidates moved to Obama's left, argue Ezra Klein and Roge Karma in the liberal outlet Vox:

The Democratic Party's shift to the left is multicausal. Some of it reflects Obama's accomplishments: his achievements are a foundation the 2020 candidates are building on. Some of it reflects the changed realities the candidates are responding to—climate change has accelerated since 2008, the student debt crisis has worsened, and Donald Trump's presidency has transformed the domestic political context, particularly on immigration. And some of it reflects the influence Sanders and a resurgent left have had on the entire Democratic Party.

Still, while the 2020 primary is being touted as an ideological battle for the future of the Democratic Party, in many ways, the future of the Democratic Party is already here.

But Democrats are still uneasy about placing the party's future in the hands of Joe Biden. He is seen as a figure from the past, the bumbling senator who just happened to become Barack Obama's vice president, a position in which he failed to distinguish himself.

Biden likes to say that he is proud of his vice presidency and his role in the Obama administration. He goes on about its supposedly pristine record: "Know what I was most proud of? For eight years, there wasn't one single hint of a scandal or a lie."

That, of course, is a lie. Siraj Hashmi, writing for the *Washington Examiner*, enumerates multiple scandals that occurred under Obama and Biden, including the use of the IRS to harass conservative activists: "In 2013, an IRS official admitted the agency was aggressively scrutinizing groups with names such as 'Tea Party' or 'Patriots.' It was later reported that the IRS stepped up this scrutiny against conservative groups starting in 2010 when applications for tax-exempt status surged. Conservatives charged the Obama administration with weaponizing the IRS against his political opponents."[9]

According to Biden, Obama didn't endorse him at the beginning of the Democratic primaries because Biden asked him not to. "I want to earn this on my own," Biden said. "I have no doubt when I'm the nominee he'll be out on the campaign trail for me."

"The truth might be more complicated," wrote Hunter DeRensis of the *National Interest*. "Despite the public adulation of each other, behind the scenes of the Obama presidency the two men had a more stressed relationship. When Barack Obama chose Biden, a man twenty years his senior who had just concluded his second failed presidential campaign, to be on his ticket, it was because he did not want to deal with an internecine succession battle. This still almost came to pass in 2016, when Biden mulled a late challenge to Hillary Clinton. Obama was one of several people to quietly talk him out of it."[10]

For Donald Trump, the explanation for Obama's hesitancy is even simpler: "He knows something [about Biden] that you don't."

CHAPTER 16

The Biden Family Business: Corruption

During his long senatorial career, Joe Biden cast himself as an everyman, "Amtrak Joe," known for taking the train daily to Washington, D.C., from his home in Delaware. The image he sought to create was one of a simple legislator independent of the usual corrupting influences pols face.

In truth, Joe Biden knows those influences all too well. He heads up a family of wealthy lobbyists and political operatives who have spent decades trading on his last name.

In *Profiles in Corruption*, Peter Schweizer points out that the Biden family's wealth "depends on Joe Biden's political influence and involves no less than five family members: Joe's son Hunter, daughter Ashley, brothers James and Frank, and sister Valerie."[1]

Biden's sister has headed up a political messaging firm, to which "two and a half million dollars flowed . . . from Citizens for Biden and Biden for President Inc. during the 2008 presidential bid alone," Schweizer wrote.[2]

Meanwhile, Biden's brothers have capitalized on his public "service" through a variety of lobbying gigs and sketchy businesses. Hunter Biden got a million-dollar job on the board of a Ukrainian natural gas firm without a lick of experience in that field.[3] And Biden's brother James became an executive at a construction firm even though he had little to no experience in construction, according to Schweizer: "James Biden was joining Hillstone just as the firm was starting negotiations to win a massive contract in war-torn Iraq."[4]

Brother Frank, though he had no experience in education, used his last name to get a job with a dubious charter school management firm that raked in millions of dollars from federal grants during the Obama years—all while his brother feigned opposition to such expenditures.[5]

"It would be easier to dismiss these entanglements if they only involved one of the Bidens," writes Schweizer. "The fact that it involves five family members indicates that there is a culture within the Biden family that trades off Joe's power. And Joe appears willing to act on their behalf whenever he can."[6]

Even leftists find the Biden's family record embarrassing. Branko Marcetic of *Jacobin* magazine wrote of his fears of a Biden candidacy: "The Biden family's propensity for engaging in money-making ventures that—gee whiz, just somehow seem to constantly overlap with Biden's political career—will make him a perfect foil to Trump. Whether it's Biden's son, Hunter, being hired as a lobbyist for a Delaware credit card company whose favored legislation Biden was voting for; Biden's brother mysteriously getting hired by a mid-size construction firm shortly before it received a $1.5 billion government contract; or Hunter, again, joining the board of a corruption-tainted Ukrainian gas producer while Biden spearheaded US policy on Ukraine."[7]

Politico's Ben Schreckinger refers to the family as Biden Inc: "Biden's image as a straight-shooting man of the people, however, is clouded by the careers of his son and brother, who have lengthy track records of making, or seeking, deals that cash in on his name. There's no evidence that Joe Biden used his power inappropriately or took action to benefit his relatives with respect to these ventures. Interviews, court records, government filings and news reports, however, reveal that some members of the Biden family have consistently mixed business and politics over nearly half a century, moving from one business to the next as Joe's stature in Washington grew."[8]

Critics also note another source of political corruption over the years: Biden's closeness with credit card companies in Delaware. "Joe Biden pretends that he is middle-class Joe and in reality he's corporate Joe," Georgetown Law professor Adam Levitin told the *Washington Examiner.*[9]

Biden did the bidding of the credit card industry most famously by spearheading the 2005 Bankruptcy Abuse Prevention and Consumer Protection Act, which put the squeeze on consumers. The Delaware-based credit card company MBNA, which had dumped tens of thousands of dollars into Biden's campaign chest over the years, lobbied hard for the bill. Biden's subservience to the company inspired reporter Byron York to give him the nickname "the senator from MBNA."[10]

Raw political self-interest, not moderate ideology, drove his decision to push legislation for credit card companies. "The bill was a big, fat, wet kiss for credit card companies and auto lenders," Levitin told the *Washington Examiner.*[11]

Liberals hold the 2005 legislation against Biden to this day. "His energetic work on behalf of the credit card companies has earned him the affection of the banking industry and protected him from any well-funded challengers for his Senate seat," Elizabeth Warren wrote for the *Harvard Women's Law Journal.* "This important part of Senator Biden's legislative work also appears to be missing from his Web site and publicity releases."

The liberal publication *Mother Jones* noted, "Biden takes criticism of his bankruptcy position personally, in part because it infringes so directly on his well-cultivated political identity—a middle-class warrior and longtime critic of corporate campaign contributions."[12]

The liberal HuffPost also expressed disappointment in Biden for not standing up for the little guy: "During his career as a senator, Biden also supported many policies that were favorable to banks and big corporations, such as legislation exempting soda makers from antitrust regulation and financial deregulatory measures that helped set the stage for the 2008 financial crisis and Great Recession."[13]

Fordham Law professor Zephyr Teachout is another liberal who thinks Biden's corruption makes him eminently defeatable: "Biden has a big corruption problem and it makes him a weak candidate. . . . 'Middle Class' Joe has perfected the art of taking big contributions, then representing his corporate donors at the cost of middle- and working-class Americans. Converting campaign contributions into legislative favors and policy positions isn't being 'moderate.' It is the kind of transactional politics Americans have come to loathe."[14]

Over the years Biden has portrayed himself as nearly penniless. In fact, he is a multimillionaire.

"The 77-year-old has touted himself as 'Middle-Class Joe' for decades—but he and his wife, Jill, have a net worth of $9 million, according to a Forbes estimate from July 2019," wrote Taylor Borden of Business Insider. "The couple's fortune is mostly tied to public speaking engagements and book royalties, according to tax returns and financial disclosures released by the Biden campaign and published on the campaign's website."[15]

Biden's friendly relationship with MBNA during his senatorial years resulted in a gusher of benefits for him and his family, as Byron York established in a piece about that relationship in the *American Spectator*: "Biden and MBNA have indeed developed a pretty cozy relationship. John Cochran, the company's vice-chairman and chief marketing officer, did pay top dollar for Biden's house, and MBNA gave Cochran a lot of money—$330,000—to help with 'expenses' related to the move. A few months after the sale, as Biden's re-election effort got under way, MBNA's top executives contributed generously to his campaign in a series of coordinated donations that sidestepped the limits on contributions by the company's political action committee. And then, a short time after the election, MBNA hired Biden's son for a lucrative job in which, according to bank officials, he is being groomed for a senior management position."[16]

Despite all of this, Biden has made removing money from politics one of his signature issues. He has hypocritically bashed the Trump family for enriching themselves off the government while exonerating his own son and siblings from that charge.

He says that he "strongly believes that we could improve our politics overnight if we flushed big money from the system and had public financing of our elections. Democracy works best when a big bank account or a large donor list are not prerequisites for office, and elected representatives come from all backgrounds, regardless of resources. But for too long, special interests and corporations have skewed the policy process in their favor with political contributions."

Biden's campaign website says that he has "advocated for public financing of federal campaigns since the very beginning of his Senate career. He first co-sponsored legislation to create a public financing system for House and Senate candidates in 1973. In 1997 and many years afterward, he co-sponsored a constitutional amendment that would have limited contributions as well as corporate and private spending in elections and prevented the damage caused by the Supreme Court in *Citizens United*."

Yet from the very beginning of his career Biden used his political activities to benefit his family. According to *The Atlantic*, even "some of his aides" worried about the appearance of "impropriety" that caused: "His family members started working for him during his first campaign, a 1970 run for New Castle County council. His sister, Valerie Biden Owens, managed that council race and his first Senate run two years later. His brother Jimmy handled fundraising for that Senate run. His other brother, Frank, was the volunteer coordinator."[17]

The Center for Public Integrity did a report on Biden and found him to be the typical money-grubbing pol who leverages his associations to benefit himself, his family, and his former aides:

> In the past couple of years, Biden has created a network of
> organizations across the country that employ his former

political aides—a savvy move, some said, for a politician preparing for a potential presidential run, according to the *New York Times*. They include American Possibilities (a political action committee), the Beau Biden Foundation for the Protection of Children, the Biden Cancer Initiative, Biden Foundation, Biden Institute, and the Penn Biden Center for Diplomacy and Global Engagement. . . .

Notable donors to American Possibilities PAC, according to Federal Election Commission filings, include Timothy Gill, a Colorado software entrepreneur and gay-rights activist; Hollywood producers Steven Spielberg and Jeffrey Katzenberg; Joe Kiani, CEO of healthcare technology company Masimo Corp. and chairman of Masimo Foundation; and Larry Rasky, chairman and CEO of public relations firm Rasky Partners, who also served as Biden's press secretary for his presidential bid in 1988 and communications director for "Biden for President" during the 2008 presidential race. Biden dropped out of the 2008 race after winning less than 1 percent of the vote during the first-in-the-nation Iowa caucus.

The Biden Foundation raked in $3.2 million in 2017, according to the nonprofit's latest tax return. Over a longer period, the foundation received at least $1 million each from its top three donors, which are disclosed on the organization's website: Gill and his husband, Scott Miller; the Masimo Foundation; and the Bohemian Foundation, a community oriented nonprofit based in Fort Collins, Colorado.[18]

None of this stops Biden from pontificating about "dark money" and other evil influences in politics.

As we have seen, he has made the ludicrous claim that the Obama administration was scandal-free: "For the eight years of the Obama-Biden Administration, there was not a hint of scandal. The administration established the most stringent ethics code ever adopted by any White House. Its procedures ensured that all decisions were made on the merits, without bias, favoritism, or undue influence.... The Trump Administration has shredded those standards. Trump is accepting foreign emoluments, and has disregarded his pledge not to expand his business overseas. And, Trump is using the federal government to prop up his resorts with countless tax dollars."

Biden's moralizing about Trump never seems to stop. He even says that Trump is "corrupting" America's children—this from a pol whose son Hunter is a walking display of corruption. The irony of fretting over the "example" Trump is setting for the nation's children while his own child self-destructs appears to be lost on Biden.

Hunter Biden has had serious drug problems, a habit he has financed with money from his lucrative gigs in Ukraine and China. The Intercept's Ryan Grim reports, "One particularly out-of-control bender, which included a crack pipe found in a rental car, took place while Biden was making $50,000 a month serving on the board of [the Ukrainian company] Burisma."[19]

In 2020, Hunter Biden got hit with a paternity suit by a woman in Arkansas. Then there are his Ashley Madison troubles: Hunter's name turned up in the subscriber data for the dating site for adulterers after it got hacked. Hunter tried to explain it away as a dirty trick by the Russians. But reporter Patrick Howley traced the breached subscriber data back to the university where Hunter was teaching: "[A]ccount information shows that the profile, which was confirmed by a credit card purchase in 2014, was used at the latitude/longitude point of 38.912682, -77.071704. That latitude-longitude point just happens to exist on the Georgetown University campus, at an administrative building on Reservoir Road. And Hunter Biden just happened to be teaching there around the time the account was set up."[20]

A bad influence on Hunter was his lobbyist uncle, James Biden, who has been cashing in on his brother's last name for years, according to reporter Ryan Grim: "In trading on his father's name and power to advance his career, Hunter Biden is following in the footsteps of James Biden, Joe's younger brother."

At one point, Hunter and his uncle worked for the same phony-baloney financial firm—that is, until Paradigm Global Advisors went bust in 2010.[21]

According to the *New Yorker*, Hunter has been to rehab at least five times and once had a crack dealer pull a gun on him. After testing positive for cocaine use, he got bounced from the Navy Reserve.[22]

His cavortings have proven particularly messy. Hunter got sexually involved with his dead brother's wife, then crossed the country to live in Los Angeles after the relationship dissolved, only to enter into a quickie wedding with a South African woman he had known for less than two weeks. ABC reported that Joe Biden, after learning of the spontaneous wedding, told his son's freshly minted wife, "Thank you for giving my son the courage to love again"—a line so laughable only the tacky Joe Biden could have come up with it.[23]

Hunter Biden makes Hugh and Tony Rodham, Hillary's buffoonish loose-living brothers, look abstemious. And yet even Hunter is given to moralizing about Trump. He has decried what the supposedly amoral Donald Trump has "done to the presidency." Hunter has said he was taught by his pop to "revere" the office, and it makes him really, really sad to see it fall into the hands of such a vulgarian.[24]

Such commentary is remarkable given the role Hunter's father has played in protecting his corrupt ventures. One interesting question is what role Biden played in protecting Hunter's lucrative job in Ukraine. As John Solomon reported in *The Hill* in 2019:

> Joe Biden couldn't resist the temptation last year to brag to an audience of foreign policy specialists about the time as vice president that he strong-armed Ukraine into firing its top prosecutor. . . .
>
> But Ukrainian officials tell me there was one crucial piece of information that Biden must have known but didn't mention to his audience: The prosecutor he got fired was leading a wide-ranging corruption probe into the natural gas firm

Burisma Holdings that employed Biden's younger son, Hunter, as a board member.[25]

Joe Biden's campaign website has a section on what he would do to curb lobbying. In light of his family's involvement in dubious lobbying, the section looks like overcompensation on Biden's part:

HOLD THE LOBBIED AND LOBBYISTS TO A HIGHER STANDARD OF ACCOUNTABILITY

Our government should operate in the public interest—making decisions on the merits, and not to meet the demands of well-heeled interests. The public has a right to know when lobbyists meet Members of Congress and Executive Branch officials; it should know with whom they speak, and about what. What's more, lobbyists often provide draft legislative or regulatory language they hope to be enacted. That information should be made public, too. Today, our lobbyist regulations are filled with loopholes and only lobbyists and the corporate interests they represent are required to disclose far too little. It is time that we strengthen our lobbyist rules and hold public officials accountable by making sure they meet these higher standards too.

As president, Biden will:

- Hold elected officials accountable for public transparency of lobbying meetings. Existing lobbying law focuses primarily on the people who are doing the lobbying. It is time the law expanded to include the public officials who are the subject of lobbying. If your Senator or Representative is meeting with a special interest group, you should know. If the Secretary of Education is making decisions about student debt after dozens of meetings with lenders, you should know that, too. Biden will expand lobbying disclosure laws, so the obligation for transparency falls on the office-holder, as well as on the lobbyist. Specifically, Biden will propose legislation to require elected officials to disclose monthly any meetings or communications with any lobbyist or special interest trying to influence the passage or defeat of a specific bill—whether seeking the office-holder's vote, or assistance in introducing or developing legislation. Under the Biden plan, members of Congress will be required to disclose any legislative language or bill text submitted by any lobbying party. Executive Branch officials will be required to disclose any regulatory text submitted by any outside entity. And, members of Congress and senior executive branch officials will be required to develop and disclose any access policy they have that governs requests for appointments. The CFE will make all of that information publicly available. If an office-holder believes that meetings with particular entities serve the public, let them explain why.

• Make lobbying disclosure meaningful. Lobbying law should effectively inform the public and discourage conduct that distorts government decision-making. But current law does neither. Disclosure requirements are riddled with loopholes, so lobbyists can coordinate a PR campaign without ever disclosing their work. Detailed campaigns can be shielded by vague references to lobbying a chamber of Congress. Influencers are free to disclose only general information about the laws and regulatory activity they are trying to shape, without revealing specifics. Biden will lower the threshold for when those seeking to influence government decisions must register as "lobbyists"—to include anyone who earns more than $1,000 annually to be involved in developing or overseeing a lobbying strategy. The law will require them to disclose in detail exactly what they're doing: with whom they're meeting, the materials they're sharing, any specific legislative (or regulatory) language they are proposing, and precisely what outcomes they're seeking.

- Prohibiting foreign governments' use of lobbyists. There is no reason why a foreign government should be permitted to lobby Congress or the Executive Branch, let alone interfere in our elections. If a foreign government wants to share its views with the United States or to influence its decision-making, it should do so through regular diplomatic channels. The Biden Administration will bar lobbying by foreign governments; and it will require that any foreign business seeking to lobby must verify that no foreign government materially owns or controls any part of it.

- Ensure truly public access. In Washington, the ability to schedule a meeting with an elected official or his or her staff is a form of currency. Under the Biden plan, members of Congress and senior Executive Branch officials will be required to develop and disclose to the public any policies that their office has instituted on when to accept or prioritize appointments. In addition, Biden will return to the Obama-Biden Administration practice of disclosing White House visitor lists.[26]

Should Biden win the presidency, would he apply any of this to his own family?

CHAPTER 17

Counterfeit Catholicism

John F. Kennedy was a checkered Catholic, to say the least. But most Catholics didn't know that or didn't care, and they voted enthusiastically for him. The checkered Catholics in today's Democratic Party can't count on the same level of support. While the liberal bishops are still in the tank for them, members of the laity and a few brave priests have wised up to their lies. Ironically, in recent years the non-Catholic Obama won the Catholic vote while heterodox Catholics such as John Kerry lost it.[1] Hillary Clinton added Tim Kaine, who wore his "social justice" Catholicism on his sleeve, to the ticket, and she ended up losing the Catholic vote in crucial states to Trump and Pence, a Catholic turned evangelical.[2]

Now it is Joe Biden who has a serious Catholic problem. On almost every moral issue he stands against the teachings of his Church. On the most important issue, abortion, he has gone completely to the other side. At one time he seemed to support abortion only reluctantly. "I'm prepared to accept that at the moment of conception there's human life and being," Biden told the Jesuit magazine *America*. "But I'm not prepared to say that to other God-fearing, non-God-fearing people that have a different view."[3]

These days Biden brags about his 100 percent rating from NARAL and promises feminists that protecting abortion rights will be one of the top priorities of his administration. He is also a loud proponent of embryonic stem cell research, another position in open defiance of Church teaching.

"I hear all this talk about how the Republicans are going to work in dealing with parents who have both the joy, because there's joy to it as well, the joy and the difficulty of raising a child who has a developmental disability, who were born with a birth defect. Well guess what folks? If you care about it, why don't you support stem cell research?" Biden has said.[4]

His reversal on the Hyde Amendment, which prohibits taxpayer funding for abortion, is Biden's final affront to Catholics. Biden has in effect declared himself to be a bad Catholic and is increasingly treated as such by Church figures. During the 2020 primaries, in an incident foreshadowing many similar ones to come, he was denied the Eucharist at a parish down in South Carolina.[5] Biden had hoped the incident would go unreported. It didn't. The priest, Fr. Robert Morey, went public, saying, "Sadly, this past Sunday, I had to refuse Holy Communion to former Vice President Joe Biden. Holy Communion signifies we are one with God, each other and the Church. Our actions should reflect that. Any public figure who advocates for abortion places himself or herself outside of Church teaching."[6]

The priest's position is unassailably rooted in Church law, but, naturally, the liberal bishops kneecapped him. New York's Cardinal Timothy Dolan, who has all the sturdiness of a tower of jelly, said that he wouldn't have denied Biden Communion. Biden's own bishop, Wilmington's Francis Malooly, also announced that he would give Biden Communion.[7]

All of this was predictable. Less predictable was Biden's muted response, which is a clear indication that his handlers have told him that these Communion controversies hurt him politically. The hopelessly biased

Judy Woodruff of PBS gave Biden an opportunity to play the victim. In answer to a softball question from Woodruff, Biden claimed that "it is a private matter." But Biden being Biden, he couldn't help adding the whopper, "It is not a position I have found anywhere else."[8] That is nonsense; plenty of priests and a few bishops have said that they would deny him Communion. The name-dropping Biden also couldn't stop himself from invoking Pope Francis and noting that he "gives me Communion."[9] (Biden was friendly with one prelate whom he doesn't mention anymore, former cardinal Theodore McCarrick, the rapist who has been laicized. McCarrick was a concelebrant at the funeral of Biden's son Beau.)[10]

Biden and the pope appear to share a socialist interpretation of Catholicism: "I was raised in a tradition called Catholic social doctrine. It is that is legitimate to look out for yourself, but never at the expense of someone else. It is legitimate to do well, but never at the expense of not looking at what is behind you. We need to create a culture which, as Pope Francis reminds us, cannot just be based on the worship of money. We cannot accept a nation in which billionaires compete as to the size of their super-yachts. . . ."[11]

Such claims won't solve his Catholic problem. For one thing, invoking Pope Francis plays poorly in American politics, as the opponents of Donald Trump found out in 2016. Trump's poll numbers didn't fall but rose after the pope slammed his immigration position.[12] Hiding behind an obnoxious left-wing pope won't help Biden any more than it helped Hillary and Kaine, who tried to drive that same wedge between Trump and Catholic voters. Kaine's faux-Catholic schtick—he regularly went on and on about his Jesuit Volunteer Corps work in Latin America with communists—went over like a lead balloon.

The Catholics who bother to go to Mass regularly anymore are loath to vote for a candidate who supports abortion in all its grisly stages and presides over gay weddings (as Biden has done since pushing Barack Obama to support gay marriage in 2012). These positions pose an insuperable impediment to picking up Catholic votes. Notice that Biden recites his I-grew-up-Catholic-in-Scranton lines less and less. His strategists have probably concluded that that routine will only remind people of his checkered Catholicism in the general election. His "private" Catholic stances grow fainter and fainter and can't even be found in a penumbra.

There was a time when the Mario Cuomos used to say that they were "personally opposed" to abortion. These days that rhetoric would ruin Catholic Democrats in the primaries. They can't even say that they want abortion safe, legal, and rare, Bill Clinton's trope. Rank-and-file Dems would call them cowards for using that language. The base wants abortion safe or unsafe, legal to the hilt, and as common as aspirin.

Even if Biden tacks to the middle in the general election, he is marked by a stain of pro-abortion extremism that can't be expunged. We can only hope more priests follow Church law and ban him from Communion, thus reminding Americans across the country that his self-described, nostalgia-ridden Catholicism is a crock.

Biden's Pitch to Left-Wing Catholics

Nevertheless, Biden is competing for the Catholic vote in his own way. His campaign website lays out "Joe Biden's Agenda for the Catholic Community." But this pitch for the Catholic vote contains no distinctively Catholic issues. It is simply a reiteration of his leftist agenda:

> Vice President Joe Biden believes that in America, no matter where you start in life, everyone should be able to live up to their God-given potential. He knows that we need to rebuild the middle class, and this time make sure everybody comes along—regardless of race, gender, religion, sexual orientation, or disability.
>
> Build an economy where everyone comes along and we protect the "least of these": Joe is running for President to rebuild the backbone of America—the middle class—and this time to make sure everyone comes along. Joe knows that the

middle class isn't a number—it's a set of values. Owning your home. Sending your kids to college. Being able to save and get ahead. Across the country, for too many families that's out of reach. The next president needs to understand what the current one doesn't: In America, no matter where you start in life, there should be no limit to what you can achieve. Toward this end, Joe will increase the federal minimum wage to $15. He will triple Title I funding to eliminate the funding gap between high- and low-income school districts as well as invest in community colleges and training to improve student success and grow a stronger, more prosperous, and more inclusive middle class. He will pay for these investments in working Americans by making sure the super-wealthy and corporations pay their fair share. His first step will be reversing President Trump's tax cuts for the super-wealthy and corporations. Joe will also eliminate special tax breaks that reward special interests and get rid of the capital gains loophole for multi-millionaires.

Respect the dignity of work and give workers back the power to earn what they're worth: The American middle class built this country. Yet today, CEOs and Wall Street are putting profits over workers, plain and simple. It's wrong. There used to be a basic bargain in this country that when you work hard, you were able to share in the prosperity your work helped create. It's time to restore the dignity of work and give workers back the power to earn what they're worth. Joe will start by strengthening unions and helping workers bargain successfully for what they deserve. His plan will check the abuse of corporate power over labor and hold corporate executives personally accountable for violations of labor laws. He will also encourage and incentivize unionization and collective bargaining. And importantly, he will ensure that workers are treated with dignity and receive the pay, benefits, and workplace protections they deserve. That means standing up against wage suppression through non-compete clauses, and stopping companies from classifying low wage workers as managers in order to avoid paying them the overtime they've earned. Finally, working- and middle-class Americans deserve to retire with dignity, so Joe will put Social Security on a path to long-run solvency, protect widows and widowers from steep Social Security benefit cuts, provide a higher Social Security benefit for the oldest Americans, and protect and strengthen Medicare and ensure its beneficiaries can access home and community long-term care when they want it.

Ensure that affordable, quality health care is a right for all Americans: Joe knows there's no peace of mind if you cannot afford to care for a sick child or family member because of a pre-existing condition, because you've reached a cap on your health insurance coverage, or because you have to make a decision between putting food on the table or going to the doctor. He will expand coverage and lower health care costs by protecting and building upon Obamacare. This includes giving Americans a public health insurance option, increasing the value of tax credits to lower premiums, and expanding coverage to low-income Americans. He will also put a stop to runaway drug prices and the profiteering of the drug industry.

Pursue a humane immigration policy that keeps families together, strengthens our economy, and secures our border: As vice president, Joe backed comprehensive immigration reform, and the Obama-Biden Administration took historic steps to create the DACA program so DREAMers could pursue their lives free from fear of deportation. Joe also led the administration's work with Central America—securing $750 million to boost prosperity and security in El Salvador, Guatemala, and Honduras, easing the root causes of migration. As president, Joe will prioritize a comprehensive immigration reform to finally give 11 million undocumented immigrants a roadmap to citizenship. He'll invest in smart technology at our ports of entry and streamline the asylum system, hiring more immigration judges. He'll ensure those seeking refuge in the United States are treated with dignity and get the fair hearing they're legally entitled to. Moreover, a Biden Administration will extend TPS to Venezuelans seeking relief from humanitarian crisis, and will immediately review and overturn every TPS decision made by the Trump Administration that does not appropriately consider the facts on the ground.

Serve as stewards of our creation and protect our planet against climate change: In his encyclical *Laudato Si*, Pope Francis directed the global community to raise awareness about the growing climate change crisis. Climate change threatens communities across the country, from beachfront coastal towns to rural farms in the heartland. Joe's plan will tackle climate change and pollution to protect our communities. He will ensure that communities harmed by climate change and pollution, particularly communities of color and low-income communities, are the first to benefit from his clean economy revolution. He will push the United States to achieve a 100 percent clean energy economy and reaches net zero emissions no later than 2050. Joe's plan will create 10 million good-paying jobs in the United States, hold polluters accountable, and push other countries to go further on their climate action commitments. He will work to ensure that every American has access to clean drinking water, clean air, and an environment free from pollutants. And, every dollar spent towards rebuilding infrastructure will be used to prevent, reduce, and withstand a changing climate.[13]

None of this constitutes authentic outreach to Catholics. It constitutes outreach to left-wingers who happen to be Catholic. It is essentially an appeal to bad Catholics.

Mass-going Catholics should expect nothing from Biden. Actually, worse than nothing. They should expect Biden to persecute them in the same way that Obama did. Recall Obama's lawsuit against the Little Sisters of the Poor. The "Catholic" Biden will renew such suits should he win the presidency. The "Catholic" Biden would preside over the grimmest of ironies: an anti-Catholic Catholic presidency.

CHAPTER 18

The Flip-Flopper

Joe Biden used to take a tough stand on drugs.[1] It was one of the policy positions that contributed to his reputation as a "moderate." But Biden jettisoned that position as he pandered to the far left of the Democratic Party during the 2020 primaries.

Today's Democrats present themselves as both the party of health and the party of drug legalization. Biden has adopted this incoherent position as his own.

He now takes a decidedly soft approach to the issue of drugs. From his campaign website:

- End, once and for all, the federal crack and powder cocaine disparity. The Obama-Biden Administration successfully narrowed the unjustified disparity between crack and powder cocaine sentences. The Biden Administration will eliminate this disparity completely, as then-Senator Biden proposed in 2007. And, Biden will ensure that this change is applied retroactively.

- Decriminalize the use of cannabis and automatically expunge all prior cannabis use convictions. Biden believes no one should be in jail because of cannabis use. As president, he will decriminalize cannabis use and automatically expunge prior convictions. And, he will support the legalization of cannabis for medical purposes, leave decisions regarding legalization for recreational use up to the states, and reschedule cannabis as a schedule II drug so researchers can study its positive and negative impacts.

- End all incarceration for drug use alone and instead divert individuals to drug courts and treatment. Biden believes that no one should be imprisoned for the use of illegal drugs alone. Instead, Biden will require federal courts to divert these individuals to drug courts so they receive treatment to address their substance use disorder. He'll incentivize states to put the same requirements in place. And, he'll expand funding for federal, state, and local drug courts.

Biden once called marijuana a "gateway drug."[2] Now he says, "I don't think it is a gateway drug. There's no evidence I've seen to suggest that."[3]

Biden has come a long way since criticizing George H. W. Bush's war on drugs as too soft: "Quite frankly, the President's plan is not tough enough, bold enough, or imaginative enough to meet the crisis at hand. In a nutshell, the President's plan does not include enough police officers to catch the violent thugs, enough prosecutors to convict them, enough judges to sentence them, or enough prison cells to put them away for a long time."[4]

Imagine Biden making such a statement these days.

His reversal on the Hyde Amendment—the ban on taxpayer funding for abortion—also sheds light on his character. Even some liberal commentators couldn't believe that flip-flop. Chris Cillizza of CNN wrote,

The abruptness of the reversal on Hyde suggests two things about Biden's position—and the campaign going forward:

1) It can't have been all that deeply held and based on his personal faith if he abandoned it after 48 hours of moderate pressure from liberal interest groups.

2) He's conscious of—and concerned about—the left rebelling against him, and is willing to bend past positions (and do so quickly) in order to get out of the firing range of these liberals.[5]

Richard Cohen of the *Washington Post* wrote a piece entitled "Joe Biden's Flip Flop Reeks of Insincerity," pointing out that the reversal spoke to Biden's political cowardice: "It's troubling that Biden should so easily abandon what, until the other day, seemed a deeply held position. It is also troubling that a major element of the Democratic Party is so intolerant of an opposing idea that it would doom a candidacy on that basis alone. This lockstep abortion platform seeks to impose a simplistic position on a morally vexing issue and is reminiscent of 1992, when at the Democratic National Convention, the party denied a pro-life Democrat, Gov. Robert P. Casey Jr. of Pennsylvania, a speaking slot."[6]

Another Biden flip-flop involves health care for illegal immigrants. "Joe Biden is now doing what Democrats always do when asked to defend their stance on immigration: He's pretending he doesn't support the thing he just advocated," said Eddie Scarry in the *Washington Examiner* in July 2019. "All the Democrats on stage at the second Democratic debate last week, including Biden, raised their hands to affirm that their healthcare plans 'would provide coverage' for illegal immigrants. But in an interview that aired Friday on CNN, Biden tried desperately to pretend that's not his position, while still maintaining that there would be free health care for illegal immigrants (though he'd rather not call it that)."[7]

An even bigger flip-flop involves Biden's position on bankruptcy reform. He now says that he supports Elizabeth Warren's position on the issue—after having opposed it for years. His campaign website says:

> Biden is adopting Senator Warren's comprehensive proposal, Fixing Our Bankruptcy System to Give People a Second Chance. In 2005, Biden worked hard to add progressive reforms to a bankruptcy bill that was going to be passed with or without him. Today, he agrees firmly with Senator Warren that we need to fundamentally reshape our bankruptcy system.
>
> As described by Senator Warren in her plan, this plan will:
>
> - Make it easier for people being crushed by debt to obtain relief through bankruptcy.
> - Expand people's rights to take care of themselves and their children while they are in the bankruptcy process.
> - End the absurd rules that make it nearly impossible to discharge student loan debt in bankruptcy.
> - Let more people protect their homes and cars in bankruptcy so they can start from a firm foundation when they start to pick up the pieces and rebuild their financial lives.
> - Help address shameful racial and gender disparities that plague our bankruptcy system.
> - Close loopholes that allow the wealthy and corporate creditors to abuse the bankruptcy system at the expense of everyone else.[8]

Matthew Yglesias of Vox explains the significance of this flip-flop:

> Paired with the promise to select a woman as his running mate, it demonstrates a clear desire on Biden's part to consolidate Warren supporters as part of his coalition.

It's also part of a larger pattern in which Biden tends to shore up his progressive bona fides not by disavowing positions he took in the past—for the Iraq War, for example—but by denying that he ever took them. It's a strategy that is obviously working for him on one level (he's winning, after all) but will make it hard for him to win the support of progressive thought-leaders and activists who pay attention to the details.[9]

Biden has also changed his tone over the years. In the 1990s, he joined Bill Clinton in moving to the middle and urging "personal responsibility." Now Biden simply panders to the lower class. Take his position on housing. "We're going to go after those people involved in gentrification," he vowed in South Carolina before its primary.

Biden has declared that "housing is a right" that the federal government has a duty to provide. "The idea that you have so many people on the street in California because of the increase in cost of housing, it's just not right, and we're gonna fully fund housing, and we're gonna make sure that everyone has access to Section 8 housing. No one should pay more than 30 percent of their income for housing," Biden has said.[10]

Biden treats housing as nothing more than an extension of his identity politics. He blames housing problems on racism:

> Communities of color are disproportionately impacted by the failures in our housing markets, with homeownership rates for Black and Latino individuals falling far below the rate for white individuals. Because home ownership is how many families save and build wealth, these racial disparities in home ownership contribute to the racial wealth gap. It is far past time to put an end to systemic housing discrimination and other contributors to this disparity.[11]

He promises to invest "$640 billion over 10 years so every American has access to housing that is affordable, stable, safe and healthy, accessible, energy efficient and resilient, and located near good schools and with a reasonable commute to their jobs."[12]

Biden sees the problem through an ideological lens. It is all about discrimination:

> Exclusionary zoning has for decades been strategically used to keep people of color and low-income families out of certain communities. As President, Biden will enact legislation requiring any state receiving federal dollars through the Community Development Block Grants or Surface Transportation Block Grants to develop a strategy for inclusionary zoning, as proposed in the HOME Act of 2019 by Majority Whip Clyburn and Senator Cory Booker. Biden will also invest $300 million in Local Housing Policy Grants to give states and localities the technical assistance and planning support they need to eliminate exclusionary zoning policies and other local regulations that contribute to sprawl.[13]

He equates standards with racism and promises to erase all the Trump-era measures designed to uphold them:

> The Obama-Biden Administration held major national financial institutions accountable for discriminatory lending practices, securing hundreds of millions of dollars in settlements to help borrowers who had been harmed by their practices. And in 2013, the Obama-Biden Administration codified a long-standing, court-supported view that lending practices that have a discriminatory effect can be challenged even if discrimination was not explicit. But now the Trump Administration is seeking to gut this disparate impact standard by significantly increasing the burden of proof for those claiming discrimination. In the Biden Administration, this change will be reversed to ensure financial institutions are held accountable for serving all customers.

Strengthen and expand the Community Reinvestment Act to ensure that our nation's bank and non-bank financial services institutions are serving all communities. The Community Reinvestment Act currently regulates banks, but does little to ensure that "fintechs" and non-bank lenders are providing responsible access to all members of the community. On top of that gap, the Trump Administration is proposing to weaken the law by allowing lenders to receive a passing rating even if the lenders are excluding many neighborhoods and borrowers. Biden will expand the Community Reinvestment Act to apply to mortgage and insurance companies, to add a requirement for financial services institutions to provide a statement outlining their commitment to the public interest, and, importantly, to close loopholes that would allow these institutions to avoid lending and investing in all of the communities they serve.

Roll back Trump Administration policies gutting fair lending and fair housing protections for homeowners. Biden will implement the Obama-Biden Administration's Affirmatively Furthering Fair Housing Rule requiring communities receiving certain federal funding to proactively examine housing patterns and identify and address policies that have a discriminatory effect. The Trump Administration suspended this rule in 2018. Biden will ensure effective and rigorous enforcement of the Fair Housing Act and the Home Mortgage Disclosure Act. And, he will reinstate the federal risk-sharing program which has helped secure financing for thousands of affordable rental housing units in partnership with housing finance agencies.

Restore the federal government's power to enforce settlements against discriminatory lenders. The Trump Administration has stripped the Office of Fair Lending and Equal Opportunity, a division of the Consumer Financial Protection Bureau, of its power to enforce settlements against lenders found to have discriminated against borrowers—for example by charging significantly higher interest rates for people of color than white individuals. Biden will return power to the division so it can protect consumers from discrimination.

Tackle racial bias that leads to homes in communities of color being assessed by appraisers below their fair value. Housing in communities primarily comprised of people of color is valued at tens of thousands of dollars below majority-white communities even when all other factors are the same, contributing to the racial wealth gap. To counteract this racial bias, Biden will establish a national standard for housing appraisals that ensures appraisers have adequate training and a full appreciation for neighborhoods and do not hold implicit biases because of a lack of community understanding. An objective national standard for appraisals will also make it harder for financial institutions to put pressure on appraisers to their benefit.[14]

Biden is the classic unprincipled pol who bends with the wind. His "moderation" was simply a function of the times. When Democrats were generally more conservative, he was more conservative. But the moment they moved to the left, he followed them. This tells us what kind of president he would be—a captive of the Democratic Party consensus. Whatever the base of the party clamors for, he will work to enact.

CHAPTER 19

The Campaign Ahead

Joe Biden has never been a good campaigner. Even his successful 2020 run in the Democratic primaries was marred by numerous blunders. The pundits gave him up for dead after he lost in Iowa and New Hampshire.[1] His eventual success had less to do with his qualities than with those of his opponents. He beat an exceedingly weak field.

Just as Bernie Sanders reaped the benefits of the anti-Hillary vote in 2016, Biden benefited from the anti-Bernie vote in 2020. Biden didn't even have to break a sweat against Bernie and company, such were their obvious weaknesses. Biden largely avoided interviews and gave short speeches, as his handlers kept him on a tight leash.

Yet even with all that obvious handling, Biden managed to get himself into some trouble. Before the Michigan primary, he called a Detroit union worker who raised concerns about his record on guns a "horse's ass" and said he was "full of shit," as we have seen.

The party elders who pulled Biden across the finish line sought to keep him out of debates. James Clyburn, the congressman who was so critical to Biden's success in South Carolina, said, "It is time for us to cancel the rest of these debates."[2]

The less Biden talks the better. "The waters parted for Joe Biden like no other candidate has ever seen," said Gloria Borger of CNN. "It's almost as if he's standing there saying, 'What? What? I'm here?' Because he did everything wrong. He lost a couple times, he came in second or third. This should not have happened, but it did happen to him."[3]

But however bumbling, Biden's campaign has filled some pundits with hopes that he can rebuild the "Blue Wall." Anything is possible, but his ugly altercation with the Detroit union worker foreshadows troubles ahead. Biden did himself no favors in the Blue Wall states by touting Beto O'Rourke as his future guns czar.[4]

Ben Mathis-Lilley of Slate, to his credit, has no illusions about Biden's success in the primaries:

> Choosing Biden was based entirely on a theory of necessity. His flaws are evident, which is why he finished fourth and fifth in Iowa and New Hampshire. He's still capable of delivering inspiring rhetoric but talks over himself, makes errors, and even becomes agitated when required to get into details. He's enthusiastic when talking about Obama's accomplishments, but presents almost no vision of what his own administration's achievements might look like.

He argues that Biden simply won by default:

> [V]oters and party leaders were unable to settle on any of the many available non-Biden, non–Bernie Sanders candidates—too young, too female, too not an actual Democrat—and have decided Sanders himself is too risky despite widespread sympathy for his goals. So it's Uncle Joe by a nose, thanks in part to the goodwill he built up under Obama and in part to all the other horses having died.

The Democrats, says Mathis-Lilley, simply see Biden as a shaky vehicle to ride back to power, one they will have to steer to the finish line and past it into the presidency:

> The Biden 2020 campaign isn't about following its nominal leader, or even listening to him; it's about the party pushing him over the line collectively—and about making plans to give him the necessary support once he's in office, as [Cory] Booker's endorsing statement alluded to in references to "winning races up and down the ballot" and thinking of a presidential victory as the "floor" rather than the "ceiling" of Democratic Party potential.[5]

Biden has taken to referring to himself as a "bridge," as if his geriatric candidacy were little more than a stopgap measure for a party bereft of leadership.[6] But Biden does have at least one advantage over the party's last candidate, Hillary Clinton. He is not nearly as reviled as she was. Then again, in Donald Trump he will be facing not a rookie candidate but an incumbent president with a record of demonstrable successes. Democrats who are reading too much into Biden's comeback against an inept field may be in for a rude shock.

Another thing that should also concern his patrons is how Biden won—by pandering to the increasingly left-wing base of the party. While Biden won the primaries, Bernie Sanders dominated the conversation within the party. Biden ended up echoing many of Sanders's positions. As Barack Obama, who took his sweet time in endorsing Biden, put it, Biden is running on the "most progressive platform" ever.

As Jeff Jacoby of the *Boston Globe* points out, Biden's contest with Sanders pushed him far to the left:

> What Biden is today is what he has always been: a liberal Democrat. But as his party has shifted left in a hyperpolarized era, Biden has shifted with it. Many of the positions he takes

that are described as centrist today, observed Axios in January, "would have been liberal dreams during the Bill Clinton years and still out of reach in the Obama era." On policy, Biden is a moderate primarily in the sense that he embraces positions that most Democrats no longer fight over.

All of which means that even if Biden wins the Democratic nomination, progressive Democrats will have reason to rejoice. Their party's standard-bearer will be someone whose platform skews further to the left than any major party platform in the past. Sanders may not end up on the November ballot, but it will unmistakably reflect his influence. For he and his band of progressives have pushed their party to the left with such success that even the "moderate" in the race would be the most liberal Democrat ever nominated for president.[7]

According to the *New York Times*, Biden reached out to the supporters of Sanders in the spring of 2020. Biden's surrogates "are striving to engage progressive Democrats who have so far been cool to Mr. Biden's presidential bid," the *Times* reported. "Mr. Biden's allies argue that the former vice president does embrace relatively bold policy—if at a more incremental pace, and on a less sweeping scale, than Mr. Sanders does. Their focus now is on promoting some of those proposals, from gun control to combating climate change, and on learning more about what supporters of other current and former candidates need to hear from Mr. Biden."[8]

Sean McElwee, co-founder of the liberal think tank Data for Progress, told *Politico*, "The dirty little secret is everyone's talking to Biden's campaign. There will be fights, but at the end of the day, progressives still hold votes in the Senate and increasingly Democratic voters stand behind our views. I expect we'll see Biden embracing key planks of the ambitious agenda progressives have outlined on issues like climate and pharmaceutical policy."[9]

Some Democratic commentators fear that Biden will be easier for Trump to beat than Sanders. "Establishment Democrats believe that by preventing a self-identified democratic socialist from winning the nomination, they are in the best possible position to win back the White House from Trump. But Biden's decades in public life not only provide the opposition with plenty of vulnerabilities to exploit, they suggest that even if he prevails, he could cripple his own presidency with an instinct to accept half a loaf on principle without even negotiating for the whole," wrote Adam Serwer of *The Atlantic*.[10]

Biden didn't win as a moderate. He won as a leftist. It is notable that in February, when his campaign was in trouble, he turned to the leftist Anita Dunn for help. Dunn is famous for having said that Chairman Mao is her favorite political philosopher.

"Former Vice President Joseph R. Biden Jr. is shaking up his campaign leadership just days ahead of the New Hampshire primary, an acknowledgment that his bid for the Democratic presidential nomination is in major trouble after a disastrous fourth-place finish in the Iowa caucuses," reported the *New York Times*. "Mr. Biden is giving effective control of the campaign to Anita Dunn, a veteran Democratic operative and top adviser to him. 'She will be working closely with us on campaign strategy and overall coordination on budget and personnel as we build a bigger campaign for the next phase,' according to a campaign email obtained by the New York Times. But two senior Biden officials said Ms. Dunn is doing more than that—and that she will have final decision-making authority, a decision that came at the behest of the former vice-president. The Biden advisers spoke on the condition of anonymity to discuss internal planning."[11]

Biden would populate his administration with left-wingers like Dunn. Progressive groups such as Justice Democrats and NextGen America have already told Biden that he must keep moderates out of his administration. Several of these organizations joined in sending him a letter demanding that he stack his administration with leftists:

Personnel and Future Administration:

- Commit to appointing progressive elected officials who endorsed Bernie Sanders or Elizabeth Warren as Transition Co-Chairs, such as Representatives Ro Khanna, Pramila Jayapal, Ayanna Pressley, or Katie Porter.
- Pledge to appoint zero current or former Wall Street executives or corporate lobbyists, or people affiliated with the fossil fuel, health insurance or private prison corporations, to your transition team, advisor roles, or cabinet.
- Appoint a trusted progressive to lead the White House Presidential Personnel Office to ensure that the entire administration is free of corruption and staffed with public servants committed to advancing a progressive agenda.
- Commit to put trusted voices on issues of importance to our generation on your campaign and transition team's policy working groups, such as Governor Inslee's policy team on climate; Senator Warren's policy team on financial regulation; Aramis Ayala, Bryan Stevenson, and Larry Krasner on criminal justice; Bonnie Castillo of National Nurses United and Dr. Abdul El-Sayed on health care; and Mary-Kay Henry, Sara Nelson, and Senator Sanders' policy team on jobs and the economy.
- Commit to appointing advisors, such as Joseph Stiglitz, to your National Economic Council and Office of Management and Budget who believe in the principles of the Green New Deal and a rapid transition to a 100% clean and renewable energy economy.
- Appoint a National Director of Gun Violence Prevention in the White House who will oversee the policy platform, coordinate across agencies, and incorporate a survivor-centered approach. Commit to appointing an Attorney General who will re-examine the Heller decision.

- Appoint a DHS Secretary committed to holding ICE and CBP agents accountable and dismantling ICE and CBP as we know them.
- Create a White House Commission to represent the voices and needs of immigrants who can work together to ensure that executive actions and legislative solutions address the needs of immigrant communities.
- Create a Task Force on Young Americans at the White House focused on the many issues unique to the next generation's health, wellbeing, and economic stability. The leadership of the office should directly report to the President and work regularly with the Domestic Policy Council, National Economic Council, and Office of Public Engagement. Taskforce representatives from each agency should be appointed by and report to respective Secretaries and taskforce leadership and focus on policy and administrative action that directly affects every aspect of young people's lives. This office should engage directly with young people across the country and ensure representation from youth movement leaders in its ranks.[12]

Such a letter could be dismissed at another time. But given the mood of the Democratic Party today, it can't be. Biden is already on record saying that he intends to fill his administration with young leftists. In April 2020, he told a group of young progressives that he would welcome them into his administration:

There are a number of people like you—and I'm not being a wise guy—who have been helping me. They're serious people who I've had discussions with about . . . asking them, are they willing to come into a government if I get elected?

And one of the ways to deal with age is to build a bench, to build a bench of younger, really qualified people who haven't had the exposure that others have had but are fully capable of being the leaders of the next four, eight, 12, 16 years to run the country. But they've got to have an opportunity to rise up.[13]

Symone Sanders, who worked for Bernie Sanders before she joined the Biden campaign as an advisor, is the prototype of the kind of leftist that will fill a Biden administration. She is a self-described "rabid feminist."

Some critics have said that Biden will fill his administration with operatives from the D.C. swamp. And those predictions are credible too. In The Daily Beast, Lloyd Green gave a preview of the kind of swamp dwellers Biden is likely to appoint to his administration—veteran Washington pol Ron Klain, for example, former chief of staff not only to Biden but also to Al Gore, and Tom Donilon (a long-in-the-tooth lawyer who has served in Democratic administrations since the days of Jimmy Carter), along with other retreads from the Obama, Clinton, and even Carter years.[14]

Ryan Lizza of *Politico* has identified members of Biden's "inner circle," including:

There's [Steven] Ricchetti, 62, the campaign chairman, former vice presidential chief of staff, former lobbyist and longtime Biden political adviser. . . .

When Biden is on the road, he is usually accompanied by Bruce Reed, 59, a Bill Clinton campaign and White House veteran who led the Democratic Leadership Council. . . .

On foreign policy, Tony Blinken, 57, who has been with Biden almost continuously since 2002, when he became Biden's staff director on the Senate Foreign Relations Committee, plays a similar role. The policy operation is overseen by Stef Feldman, an Obama veteran who has been with Biden since 2011.[15]

But who will he select to cabinet positions? The news site Axios asked the Biden campaign that question: "According to Axios, the Biden campaign is leaning toward a 'Return to Normal' plan to undo President Donald Trump's policies and reinstate much of the political apparatus that existed during the Obama years."[16]

Axios reports that the following people are under consideration:

- Former New York City mayor Mike Bloomberg for the World Bank
- Senator Elizabeth Warren of Massachusetts for Treasury secretary
- Pete Buttigieg, the former mayor of South Bend, Indiana, for US ambassador to the United Nations or the US trade representative
- Senator Kamala Harris of California or former deputy attorney general Sally Yates for attorney general
- JPMorgan Chase CEO Jamie Dimon and Bank of America vice chairman Anne Finucane for positions at the Treasury Department
- Former secretary of state John Kerry for climate change czar
- Former national security adviser Susan Rice for a State Department role

Should Biden win the presidency, we can expect his administration to house both the worst figures from the Obama years and radicals from the Bernie Sanders campaign.

During the coronavirus crisis, Biden went after Trump with increasingly weird charges. He said that he thought Trump would postpone the election, as the *New York Times* reported:

For months, Joseph R. Biden Jr. has argued that under pressure and political duress, President Trump may pursue increasingly extreme measures to stay in power.

In November, Mr. Biden said he feared that "as the walls close in on him he becomes more erratic. And I'm genuinely concerned about what he may do in order to try to hold on to the office."

In January, Mr. Biden fretted: "He still has another nine or 10 months. God knows what can happen."

And on Thursday, he added some urgency to his warnings, suggesting that Mr. Trump might try to delay or otherwise disrupt the election.

"Mark my words, I think he is going to try to kick back the election somehow, come up with some rationale why it can't be held," Mr. Biden said at a fund-raiser, according to a news media pool report. Mr. Trump, he suggested, is "trying to let the word out that he's going to do all he can to make it very hard for people to vote. That's the only way he thinks he can possibly win."[17]

Meanwhile, Biden continues to pander to the Left. As we have already seen, he announced the formation of task forces made up of his supporters and supporters of Bernie Sanders to "unify" the party. He named John Kerry and Alexandria Ocasio-Cortez to the climate change task force—an indication that his administration would combine the worst of the old Democratic Party with all the destructive radicalism of the new progressives.

Should the Next President of the United States Be Senile, Scandal-Plagued, and Racially Offensive?

ritics of Joe Biden have always questioned his judgment. But it wasn't until the 2020 race that they started to question his mental fitness. President Trump calls Biden "Sleepy Joe." Others call him "Senile Joe," noting his increasingly shaky public performances.

Trump has raised the possibility that, should he win, Biden might not even run his own administration. "[H]e's not going to be running it," Trump has said. "Other people are going to. They're going to put him into a home, and other people are going to be running the country and they're going to be super-left, radical crazies."[1]

The Trump campaign has run ads pointing to Biden's "age" and warning that "geriatric mental health is no laughing matter."[2]

But the first questions about Biden's mental fitness came from the Left, notes Glenn Greenwald of The Intercept: "Aside from the fact that Biden's cognitive decline is visible to the naked eye and it is incredibly reckless and repressive to demand that it be suppressed, these concerns were first raised not by Trump operatives nor by Sanders supporters, nor were they first raised within the last several weeks. Quite the opposite is true: they were raised repeatedly over the last year principally by Democratic Party officials and their most loyal allies in the media."[3]

Greenwald gives the example of MSNBC's Andrea Mitchell, who in 2019 asked about Biden, "[T]he question is, does he still have his stuff? How sharp is he?"[4]

Greenwald also notes Democratic congressman Tim Ryan's comment about Biden: "There's sometimes a lack of clarity, and I think that's what I'm hearing on the ground. I think that's what a lot of people are thinking, and we can't afford that at this point."[5]

Senator Cory Booker, who ran against Biden in the 2020 Democratic primaries, also suggested that Biden had lost his edge. Booker mused after one Democratic debate, "There were a lot of moments where a number of us on stage were looking at him, each other, where [Biden] tends to go on sometimes. At one point he's talking about people in communities like mine listening to record players. . . . Vinyl is hot right now, maybe he's cooler than I am, but there are definitely moments where you listen to Joe Biden and just wonder."[6]

Biden's senility was on display in May as questions arose about his role in the Michael Flynn investigation. At first Biden denied any knowledge of that investigation, only to backtrack in an interview with George Stephanopoulos of ABC, who reminded Biden that he attended a January 5, 2017, briefing on "the FBI's plan to question Michael Flynn."

Biden responded, "I thought you asked me whether or not I had anything to do with him being prosecuted. I was aware that they asked for an investigation, but that's all I know about it. I don't think anything else."[7] Shortly thereafter it came out that Biden had been one of the officials to request that Flynn's name be unmasked from the intercepted communications of foreign officials.[8]

While the media has shown no interest in the Obama administration's spying on the incoming Trump administration, Republicans in the Senate have. "I just think it's something that probably dogs Biden and his campaign for a while. The idea that they would be trying to undermine an incoming administration as late in the game as January of 2017 is pretty hard to explain," Senator John Thune has said. According to *The Hill*, "Two Senate committees are now investigating former Vice President Joe Biden's role in the 'unmasking' of former national security adviser Michael Flynn, as Republican senators seek to go on offense with an issue they think will damage the presumptive Democratic presidential nominee while helping them retain their majority."

If Biden is going to take credit for the Obama administration's successes, he will also have to take blame for its failures and scandals. Liberals are dismissing "Obamagate" as another one of Donald Trump's "conspiracy theories." Never mind that Trump has been right from the beginning about the Obama administration's spying on his campaign. James Comey sanctimoniously denied spying on Trump Tower even as spying warrants giving him the power to intercept communications there sat on his desk. And never mind that Obama's and Biden's fingerprints are all over the Flynn-related espionage.

It is impossible to overstate the anger the media would have expressed had George W. Bush pulled such stunts on the Obama campaign.

Liberals love to sanitize their own scandals. Once censorious of the CIA and FBI, they now act as if it is inconceivable that those agencies could ever abuse power, could ever spy on anyone improperly, could ever be weaponized politically. So much for liberals' ACLU-style anxieties about the civil liberties of Americans. They have shown zero sympathy for Carter Page, even though the FBI massively violated his privacy with an improperly obtained warrant. The civil libertarian Left disappears during Democratic scandals.

Liberals used to scoff at Richard Nixon's saying if a president does something it can't be illegal. But liberals' presumption about Obama and Biden is little different: if they did something, then according to the Left it can't be wrong.

Imagine if George W. Bush had participated in setting up a perjury trap for an incoming Obama official. The media furor would have been deafening. But Obama's and Biden's complicity in the Michael Flynn scandal is no big deal.

Just as Obama and Biden can do no wrong in the media's reckoning, Trump can never be right. He is the clear victim of all the baseless spying on his campaign, which led to years of unfounded harassment that hobbled his presidency. And yet the media tells us that he is wrong to complain about it. How dare he notice that he was railroaded.

Of course, many of the media figures calling Obamagate a "distraction" are buddies with its architects. John Brennan and James Clapper are retained as contributors by the very media organizations that refuse to cover their scandals. Too bad H. R. Haldeman couldn't have worked out a deal like that.

To the extent that the media covers the Obama administration's spying on the Trump campaign at all, it presents the espionage in the most innocent terms. Even something as outlandish as infiltrating Trump's campaign—the FBI sent Stefan Halper to entrap minor Trump campaign volunteers—is treated as "by the book," to borrow Susan Rice's phrase. Halper was just a "confidential informant," we're told by the media. Nothing to see there.

Again, it is impossible to overstate the anger the media would have expressed had George W. Bush pulled such stunts on the Obama campaign. It would not have been blandly described as "standard procedure" or a good-faith mistake. Some liberals have ludicrously suggested that it would have been a "dereliction of duty" if the Obama administration hadn't spied on the Trump campaign. They say this even after it has come out that much of the spying rested on a bogus dossier financed by Trump's opponent, even after the outrageous Peter Strzok texts, even after the incriminating Flynn-related documents.

Only liberals could say "we don't know what the scandal is" in the face of such facts. Their capacity for denial and projection is staggering. They spent three years accusing the U.S. government of interfering in our election, only for Americans to find out that that U.S. government was their own Democratic administration under Barack Obama. It was the John Brennans, Peter Strzoks, and James Comeys who interfered in the election. And they used foreigners to do it. Brennan and company not only made use of Hillary's British smear merchant, Christopher Steele, but also of other foreign intelligence agents—all in the service of a spying operation that never had any foundation to it and proved utterly fruitless. If you strike at a king, you better kill him. Brennan whiffed. But apparently that adage doesn't apply to liberals. They struck at a president, missed, and now demand a return to power.

We will see all the sorry players in this saga try to crawl back to influence under a Biden administration.

In May 2020, Senile Joe found himself in yet another controversy of his own making. While appearing on *The Breakfast Club*, a hip-hop radio show with a host called Charlamagne Tha God, Biden mused, "If you have a problem figuring out whether you're for me or Trump, then you ain't black."[9]

It would be difficult to imagine a more racially offensive statement. It was so bad that even Democrats joined in the condemnations of it. Congressman Jim Clyburn, one of Biden's most prominent patrons, said it made him "cringe."[10] Biden himself had to apologize, saying, "I was much too cavalier. . . . I shouldn't have been such a wise guy."[11]

This is not the first time Biden has used appalling language about black Americans. In the run-up to the 2008 election, he described Barack Obama as "the first mainstream African-American who is articulate and bright and clean and a nice-looking guy."[12]

While Biden's political career survived that outrageously insulting remark, his recent comment won't soon be forgotten. It captures perfectly the toxic identity politics he practices. It threatens to do to Biden's campaign what Hillary Clinton's "deplorables" remark did to hers.

Here's hoping that the current problems threatening to overwhelm Biden's candidacy may actually keep Joe Biden from winning his next election—unlike the countless gaffes, instances of plagiarism, and flip-flops on the issues that he has managed to bull his way through to this point.

Because this is the question of the hour: Do we really want the next president of the United States to be a Washington, D.C., swamp creature who pretends to be a moderate while actively planning to enact an agenda far to the left of any U.S. president to date—and who also happens to be seriously offensive on race, and apparently suffering from dementia?

No Longer Ready for Prime Time: Selected Recent Quotations from the Presumptive Democratic Nominee for President of the United States

"We hold these truths to be self-evident. All men and women created by the—go, you know, you know, the thing."[1]

"We have to take care of the cure. That will make the problem worse, no matter what. No matter what. We know what has to be done. We know you have to—you're tired of hearing the phrase, you got to flatten the curve where it's going up like this, people getting it, then it comes down."[2]

"You're a lying dog-faced pony soldier."[3]

"This guy [Beto O'Rourke] can change the face of what we're dealing with, with regard to guns, assault weapons, with regard to dealing with climate change. And I'm just warning Amy [O'Rourke's wife]: If I win, I'm coming for him."[4]

"If you have a problem figuring out whether you're for me or Donald Trump, then you ain't black."[5]

"You're full of shit. Now shush, shush. I support the Second Amendment. The Second Amendment—just like right now, if you yelled 'fire,' that's not free speech. And from the beginning—I have a shotgun, I have a 20-gauge, a 12-gauge. My sons hunt. Guess what? You're not allowed to own any weapon. I'm not taking your gun away, at all. You need 100 rounds?"[6]

"I would veto anything that delays providing the security and the certainty of healthcare being available now. If they got that through and by some miracle, there was an epiphany that occurred, and some miracle occurred that said OK, it's passed, then you got to look at the cost. And I want to know how did they find the $35 trillion? What is that doing?"[7]

"You know the rapidly rising umm, uh, in with, uh, with I, uh, don't know, his [Trump's] just inability to focus on any federal responsibility."[8]

"He [Trump]'s going down to Texas on Juneteenth, right? The first major massacre, literally speaking, of the, ah, black Wall Street."[9]

Acknowledgments

I would like to thank the following people for help during this project: Tom Spence, Harry Crocker, Elizabeth Kantor, Kathleen Curran, Daniel Allott, Wladyslaw Pleszczynski, R. Emmett Tyrrell Jr., Frank Walker, Scott Daily, Roger McCaffrey, Terry Kopp, Mary Neumayr, John Neumayr, and Bridget Neumayr.

Notes

Chapter 1: The Myth: Biden Is a Moderate

1. Adam Kelsey, "Joe Biden Slips, Hints at 2020 Presidential Run: 'I Have the Most Progressive Record of Anyone Running,'" ABC News, March 17, 2019, https://abcnews.go.com/Politics/joe-biden-claims-progressive-record-running-president/story?id=61660664.
2. Mike Memoli, "Joe Biden at Rally Casts Himself as Candidate Who Could Unify the Nation," NBC News, May 18, 2019, https://www.nbcnews.com/politics/politics-news/joe-biden-rally-casts-himself-candidate-who-could-unify-nation-n1007396.
3. Felicia Sonmez, "Biden Says He Would Consider Republican Running Mate, 'But I Can't Think of One Now,'" *Washington Post*, December 31, 2019, https://www.washingtonpost.com/politics/biden-says-he-would-consider-republican-running-mate-but-i-cant-think-of-one-now/2019/12/31/0c6002e2-2bfb-11ea-bcd4-24597950008f_story.html.
4. Joe Biden, *Promises to Keep* (New York: Random House, 2007), 105.
5. Richard Adams, "Joe Biden: 'This Is a Big Fucking Deal,'" *The Guardian*, March 23, 2010, https://www.theguardian.com/world/richard-adams-blog/2010/mar/23/joe-biden-obama-big-fucking-deal-overheard.

6. "ELECTION 2020—Democrats for President: Joe Biden on LGBTQ Issues," *Dallas Voice*, February 29, 2020, https://dallasvoice.com/election-2020-democrats-for-president-joe-biden-on-lgbtq-issues/.

7. Jennifer Bendery, "Joe Biden: Transgender Discrimination Is 'the Civil Rights Issue of Our Time,'" HuffPost, October 30, 2012, https://www.huffpost.com/entry/joe-biden-transgender-rights_n_2047275.

8. Ari Natter, "Biden Joins Other Democrats in Refusing to Take Money from Fossil-Fuel Industry," Bloomberg, June 29, 2019, https://www.bloomberg.com/news/articles/2019-06-29/biden-spurns-fossil-fuel-campaign-donations-in-democratic-shift.

9. Reid J. Epstein and Lisa Lerer, "Joe Biden Has Tense Exchange over L.G.B.T.Q Record," *New York Times*, September 20, 2019, https://www.nytimes.com/2019/09/20/us/politics/lgbt-forum-2020.html.

10. Quint Forgey, "How Joe Biden Would Address Criminal Justice Reform," *Politico*, July 23, 2019, https://www.politico.com/story/2019/07/23/joe-biden-criminal-justice-reform-1428017.

11. Eric Bradner and Maeve Reston, "Joe Biden Takes Trump Head-On over Charlottesville in Announcement Video," CNN, April 25, 2019, https://www.cnn.com/2019/04/25/politics/joe-biden-charlottesville-trump-2020-launch/index.html.

12. Julia Manchester, "Biden: Trump 'Encourages' White Supremacists," *The Hill*, August 8, 2019, https://thehill.com/homenews/campaign/456747-biden-trump-encourages-white-supremacy.

13. Molly Nagle and John Verhovek, "Biden Marks Anniversary of Campaign Launch with Virtual 'Soul of the Nation' Organizing Push," ABC News, April 24, 2020, https://abcnews.go.com/Politics/biden-marks-year-anniversary-campaign-launch-virtual-soul/story?id=70336462.

14. "Biden Touts Catholic Faith as Campaign Falters," Catholic News Agency, February 19, 2020, https://www.catholicnewsagency.com/news/biden-touts-catholic-faith-as-campaign-falters-65555.

15. William Cummings, "Catholic Priest Says He Denied Joe Biden Holy Communion at Mass in South Carolina Because of Abortion Views," *USA Today*, October 29, 2019, https://www.usatoday.com/story/news/politics/2019/10/29/joe-biden-denied-communion/2494025001/.

16. Lisa Lerer, "When Joe Biden Voted to Let States Overturn *Roe v. Wade*," *New York Times*, March 29, 2019, https://www.nytimes.com/2019/03/29/us/politics/biden-abortion-rights.html.

17. Branko Marcetic, "Joe Biden Is the Forrest Gump of the Democratic Party's Rightward Turn," *Jacobin*, February 27, 2020, https://www.jacobinmag.com/2020/02/joe-biden-bill-clinton-middle-class-triangulation.

18. John Verhovek, "Joe Biden: White America 'Has to Admit There's Still a Systemic Racism,'" ABC News, January 21, 2019, https://abcnews.go.com/Politics/joe-biden-white-america-admit-systemic-racism/story?id=60524966.

19. Molly Nagle and Christopher Donato, "Joe Biden Reverses Stance on Hyde Amendment," ABC News, June 6, 2019, https://abcnews.go.com/Politics/biden-reverses-stance-hyde-amendment/story?id=63538180.

20. John Verhovek and Molly Nagle, "Bernie Sanders Endorses Joe Biden, They Announce 'Working Groups' on Policy Issues," ABC News, April 13, 2020, https://abcnews.go.com/Politics/bernie-sanders-endorses-joe-biden/story?id=70123451.

21. Justine Coleman, "Biden Accuses Trump of 'All-Out Assault on the Media' during World Press Freedom Day," *The Hill*, May 3, 2020, https://thehill.com/homenews/campaign/495885-biden-accuses-trump-of-all-out-assault-on-the-media-during-world-press.

22. Quint Forgey, "Michigan Worker: Biden 'Went off the Deep End' in Expletive-Laden Exchange," *Politico*, March 11, 2020, https://www.politico.com/news/2020/03/11/michigan-worker-describes-fight-with-biden-125449.

23. Gabrielle Bruney, "The Joe Biden Allegations: Here's Everything We Know So Far," *Esquire*, April 3, 2020, https://www.esquire.com/news-politics/a27019229/joe-biden-allegations-explained/.

24. Julia Zorthian, "Joe Biden Wishes He Could Take Donald Trump 'behind the Gym,'" *Time*, October 21, 2016, https://time.com/4541405/joe-biden-take-donald-trump-behind-gym/.

25. Joe Perticone, "Flashback: Joe Biden's First Presidential Run in 1988 Cratered amid Multiple Instances of Plagiarism," Business Insider, March 12, 2019.

26. Ibid.

27. Katie Glueck, "How Biden's Campaign Explains His 'Arrest' in South Africa," *New York Times*, February 26, 2020, https://www.nytimes.com/2020/02/26/us/politics/joe-biden-arrest-mandela.html.

28. Grace Wyler, "These Photos of Joe Biden Getting Intimate with a Lady Biker Are Priceless," Business Insider, September 10, 2012, https://www.businessinsider.com/joe-biden-lady-biker-photos-2012-9.

Chapter 2: "The First Thing I Would Do Is Eliminate Trump's Tax Cut"

1. Adam Sabes, "Biden Tweet: Ignore the Fact I've Already Called for Middle Class Tax Hikes," Americans for Tax Reform, July 24, 2019, https://www.atr.org/biden-tweet-ignore-fact-i-ve-already-called-middle-class-tax-hikes.
2. Susan Jones, "'Spread the Wealth around' Comment Comes Back to Haunt Obama," CNS, October 15, 2008, https://www.cnsnews.com/news/article/spread-wealth-around-comment-comes-back-haunt-obama.
3. John Kartch, "Biden: 'If You Elect Me, Your Taxes Are Going to Be Raised,'" Americans for Tax Reform, February 29, 2020, https://www.atr.org/biden-if-you-elect-me-your-taxes-are-going-be-raised.
4. Philip Klein, "Here's a List of $6 Trillion in Joe Biden Spending Proposals," *Washington Examiner*, March 9, 2020, https://www.washingtonexaminer.com/opinion/heres-a-list-of-6-trillion-in-joe-biden-spending-proposals.
5. Michael Grunwald, "Biden Wants a New Stimulus 'a Hell of a Lot Bigger' Than $2 Trillion," *Politico*, April 25, 2020, https://www.politico.com/news/2020/04/25/joe-biden-green-stimulus-207848.
6. Kevin Breuninger, "Mike Pence Accuses Centrist Joe Biden of 'Advocating a Socialist Agenda' Like Other 2020 Democrats," CNBC, May 3, 2019, https://www.cnbc.com/2019/05/03/pence-lumps-biden-in-with-2020-democrats-advocating-a-socialist-agenda.html.
7. Paul Waldman, "Joe Biden's Surprisingly Liberal Tax Plan," *Washington Post*, December 5, 2019, https://www.washingtonpost.com/opinions/2019/12/05/joe-bidens-surprisingly-liberal-tax-plan/.
8. Andrew Wilford, "Is Joe Biden a Moderate? If You Call $2.3 Trillion in Tax Hikes Moderation," *USA Today*, February 11, 2020, https://www.usatoday.com/story/opinion/2020/02/11/joe-biden-moderate-2-3-trillion-tax-hikes-moderation-column/4682269002/.
9. Peter Suderman, "Joe Biden Is No Moderate," *Reason*, March 4, 2020, https://reason.com/2020/03/04/joe-biden-is-no-moderate/.

10. Sam Dorman, "Trump Jokes Biden Won't Be Governing As President: 'He'll Be in a Home,'" Fox News, February 29, 2020, https://www.foxnews.com/politics/trump-jokes-biden-wont-be-governing-as-president-hell-be-in-a-home.

Chapter 3: "No One Will Be Deported at All for the First 100 Days"

1. Jonathan Easley, "Biden Once Called for a Ban on Sanctuary Cities; Where Does He Stand Now?" The Hill, August 8, 2019, https://thehill.com/homenews/campaign/456638-biden-once-called-for-a-ban-on-sanctuary-cities-where-does-he-stand-now.
2. Yael Halon, "Tucker Carlson: Biden's Threat to ICE Agents Proves He's No Moderate," Fox News, January 22, 2019, https://www.foxnews.com/media/tucker-carlson-hits-back-at-biden-for-illegal-immigrant-dui-remark.
3. Andrew Arthur, "The Myth of Moderate Joe," Center for Immigration Studies, January 6, 2020, https://cis.org/Arthur/Myth-Moderate-Joe-Biden.
4. J. Edward Moreno, "Biden on Univision: Deporting 3 Million 'Was a Big Mistake,'" The Hill, February 20, 2020, https://thehill.com/homenews/campaign/483242-biden-on-univision-deporting-3-million-was-a-big-mistake.
5. "The Biden Plan for Securing Our Values as a Nation of Immigrants," Joe Biden's campaign website, https://joebiden.com/immigration/.
6. Laura Weiss, "Is Biden Going to Repeat Obama's Immigration Mistakes?" New Republic, May 12, 2020, https://newrepublic.com/article/157429/biden-going-repeat-obamas-immigration-mistakes.
7. Arthur, "The Myth of Moderate Joe."
8. Mike Lillis, "Biden: Illegal Immigrants Are Already Americans," The Hill, March 27, 2014, https://thehill.com/blogs/blog-briefing-room/news/201972-biden-illegal-immigrants-already-americans.
9. Ibid.
10. Ibid.
11. Tali Kaplan, "Tom Homan Hits back at Biden for Remark on Illegal Immigrants Arrested for DUI: He's 'Lost His Mind,'" Fox News, January 22, 2020, https://www.foxnews.com/media/tom-homan-joe-biden-illegal-immigrant-drunk-drivers.

12. Peter Kirsanow, "Joe Biden and Illegal Immigration," *National Review*, March 11, 2020, https://www.nationalreview.com/corner/joe-biden-and-illegal-immigration/.

13. Sandy Fitzgerald, "Jeh Johnson Cautions 2020 Dems: Don't Go Too Far Left," Newsmax, September 11, 2019, https://www.newsmax.com/newsfront/jeh-johnson-democrats/2019/09/11/id/932153/.

14. "The Biden Plan for Securing Our Values as a Nation of Immigrants."

15. Ibid.

16. Sean Sullivan, "Trump's New Immigration Focus Could Squeeze Biden into a Democratic Tug of War," *Washington Post*, April 21, 2020, https://www.washingtonpost.com/politics/trumps-new-immigration-focus-could-squeeze-biden-into-a-democratic-tug-of-war/2020/04/21/8f6da614-83ec-11ea-a3eb-e9fc93160703_story.html.

17. Christopher Cadelago, "Trump Licks His Chops as Biden Veers Left on Sanctuary Cities, Fracking," *Politico*, March 16, 2020, https://www.politico.com/news/2020/03/16/biden-conservatives-trump-132214.

Chapter 4: "Transgender Equality Is the Civil Rights Issue of Our Time"

1. Emily Larsen, "'Transgender Equality Is the Civil Rights Issue of Our Time': Biden Capitalizes on Bernie Sanders-Joe Rogan Blowback," *Washington Examiner*, January 25, 2020, https://www.washingtonexaminer.com/news/transgender-equality-is-the-civil-rights-issue-of-our-time-biden-capitalizes-on-bernie-sanders-joe-rogan-blowback.

2. Kitty Kelley, "Death and the All-American Boy," *Washingtonian*, June 1, 1974, https://www.washingtonian.com/1974/06/01/joe-biden-kitty-kelley-1974-profile-death-and-the-all-american-boy/.

3. Miranda Devine, "Joe Biden's Bias Comes through in Trying to Outwoke Competition: Devine," *New York Post*, https://nypost.com/2020/01/26/joe-bidens-bias-comes-through-in-tweet-devine/.

4. Brian McBride, "Vice President Joe Biden Officiated His First Wedding for Same-Sex Couple," ABC News, August 1, 2016, https://abcnews.go.com/Politics/vice-president-joe-biden-officiated-wedding-sex-couple/story?id=41058123.

5. Katie Glueck, "Joe Biden Visits Stonewall, Saying the Fight for L.G.B.T. Rights Must Continue," *New York Times*, June 18, 2019, https://www.nytimes.com/2019/06/18/us/politics/stonewall-joe-biden.html.

6. Michael Barbaro, "A Scramble as Biden Backs Same-Sex Marriage," *New York Times*, May 6, 2012, https://www.nytimes.com/2012/05/07/us/politics/biden-expresses-support-for-same-sex-marriages.html.

7. Corbett Daly, "Obama: Biden Forced Hand on Same-Sex Marriage, but 'All's Well,'" CBS News, May 10, 2012, https://www.cbsnews.com/news/obama-biden-forced-hand-on-same-sex-marriage-but-alls-well/.

8. "Joe Biden for the LGBTQ+ Community," Joe Biden's campaign website, https://joebiden.com/lgbtq/.

9. Ibid.

10. John McCormack, "A Liberal Law Professor Explains Why the Equality Act Would 'Crush' Religious Dissenters," *National Review*, May 17, 2019, https://www.nationalreview.com/2019/05/law-professor-explains-why-the-equality-act-would-crush-religious-dissenters/.

11. "The Biden Plan to Advance LGBTQ+ Equality in America and around the World," Joe Biden's campaign website, https://joebiden.com/lgbtq-policy/.

Chapter 5: "Gun Manufacturers, I'm Going to Take You On and I'm Going to Beat You"

1. Tara Law, "Beto O'Rourke's Bold Statement on Gun Control: 'Hell Yes' He Wants to Take Your AR-15," *Time*, September 13, 2019, https://time.com/5676620/beto-orourke-take-guns-ar15-ak47/.

2. Eleanor Dearman, "Beto O'Rourke, Joining Pete Buttigieg and Amy Klobuchar, Endorses Joe Biden on Eve of Super Tuesday," *USA Today*, March 3, 2020, https://www.usatoday.com/story/news/politics/elections/2020/03/03/election-beto-orourke-joe-biden-president-super-tuesday/4937075002/.

3. Lauren Frias, "Joe Biden Says He Would Institute a National Buyback Program and Reinstate the Assault Weapons Ban to 'Get Them off the Street,'" Business Insider, August 5, 2019, https://www.businessinsider.com/former-vp-joe-biden-wants-get-assault-weapons-off-streets-2019-8.

4. John Lott, "Biden, Beto, and Gun Control," *National Review*, March 4, 2020, https://www.nationalreview.com/2020/03/gun-control-joe-biden-beto-orourke-want-to-take-your-firearms/.

5. Neil Vigdor, "Bernie Sanders, Confronted on Immunity for Gun Manufacturers, Says That Was a 'Bad Vote,'" *New York Times*,

February 25, 2020, https://www.nytimes.com/2020/02/25/us/politics/
bernie-sanders-brady-bill-guns.html.

6. German Lopez, "Joe Biden's Gun Plan Calls for Universal Background
   Checks and an Assault Weapons Ban," Vox, October 2, 2019, https://
   www.vox.com/2019/10/2/20894951/joe-biden-gun-control-plan.

7. "The Biden Plan to End Our Gun Violence Epidemic," Joe Biden's
   campaign website, https://joebiden.com/gunsafety/.

8. Lawrence Keane, "Joe Biden's Plan to Come after the Firearms
   Industry," *National Review*, March 17, 2020, https://www.
   nationalreview.com/2020/03/
   joe-biden-plan-to-shut-down-the-firearms-industry/.

9. Philip Wegmann, "Biden, from Pro-Gun Senate Newbie to Gun-Control
   Gold Standard," RealClearPolitics, November 20, 2019, https://www.
   realclearpolitics.com/articles/2019/11/20/biden_from_pro-gun_senate_
   newbie_to_gun-control_gold_standard_141775.html.

10. Bo Erickson, "Joe Biden, Accused of Wanting to End 2nd Amendment,
    Responds: 'You're Full of Sh**,'" CBS News, March 10, 2020, https://
    www.cbsnews.com/news/
    biden-accused-of-wanting-to-end-2nd-amendment-responds-youre-full-
    of-shit/.

11. Lott, "Biden, Beto, and Gun Control."

Chapter 6: How Biden Will Wreck the Courts

1. Ian Millhiser, "Biden Says He'll Name a Black Woman to the Supreme
   Court. Here Are Five Names He Could Pick," Vox, March 15, 2020,
   https://www.vox.com/2020/2/25/21153824/
   biden-black-woman-supreme-court.

2. Aris Folley, "Biden Said He'd Nominate Obama to the Supreme Court If
   'He'd Take It,'" *The Hill*, December 30, 2019, https://thehill.com/
   homenews/
   campaign/476208-biden-said-hed-nominate-obama-to-the-supreme-
   court-if-hed-take-it.

3. Douglas Ernst, "Biden Not 'Satisfied' until Half of Supreme Court
   Women; Will Nominate 'Living Document' Advocates," *Washington
   Times*, December 31, 2019, https://www.washingtontimes.com/
   news/2019/dec/31/biden-not-satisfied-until-half-scotus-is-women-vow/.

4. Ibid.

5. Ibid.

6. Thomas Sowell, "A Dying Constitution," *National Review*, May 8, 2009, https://www.nationalreview.com/2009/05/dying-constitution-thomas-sowell/.

7. Dom Calicchio, "After Trump's 9th Circuit Pick Confirmed, Biden Warns of 2nd Term 'Death Grip' on Federal Courts: Report," Fox News, December 11, 2019, https://www.foxnews.com/politics/trump-could-place-death-grip-on-federal-courts-in-second-term-biden-warns-crowd-at-fundraiser.

8. Joe Biden, *Promises to Keep: On Life and Politics* (New York: Random House, 2007), 193.

9. Ibid., 187.

10. Jules Witcover, "Biden Takes Heat for Evolving Stance on Abortion," *Chicago Tribune*, June 12, 2019, https://www.chicagotribune.com/sns-201906121530—tms—poltodayctnyq-a20190612-20190612-column.html.

11. Jeffrey Rosen, "The Justice Who Believed in America," *The Atlantic*, June 27, 2018, https://www.theatlantic.com/ideas/archive/2018/06/celebrating-anthony-kennedy/563966/.

12. Devin Dwyer, "Justice Clarence Thomas Rebukes Biden-Led Confirmation Hearings in New Film," ABC News, November 28, 2019, https://abcnews.go.com/Politics/justice-clarence-thomas-rebukes-biden-led-confirmation-hearings/story?id=67235780.

13. Eddie Scarry, "Joe Biden Proves Centrist Democrats Have Lost to the Social Justice Mob," *Washington Examiner*, March 16, 2020, https://www.washingtonexaminer.com/opinion/joe-biden-proves-centrist-democrats-have-lost-to-the-social-justice-mob.

14. "Sotomayor Explains 'Wise Latina' Comment," CBS News, July 14, 2009, https://www.cbsnews.com/news/sotomayor-explains-wise-latina-comment/.

15. Ed Whelan, "Obama's 'Empathy' Standard," *National Review*, May 12, 2009, https://www.nationalreview.com/bench-memos/obamas-empathy-standard-ed-whelan-2/.

16. Lawrence Hurley, "Obama's Judges Leave Imprint on U.S. Law," Reuters, August 25, 2016, https://www.reuters.com/article/us-usa-court-obama/obamas-judges-leave-liberal-imprint-on-u-s-law-idUSKCN1110BC.

Chapter 7: Bidencare

1.   Melanie Arter, "Biden: Revamped Version of Obamacare Will Be Called Bidencare," CNS News, February 21, 2020, https://cnsnews.com/article/national/melanie-arter/biden-revamped-version-obamacare-will-be-called-bidencare.

2.   Christopher Jacobs, "3 Reasons Joe Biden's Health Care Plan Is Merely Socialism Lite," The Federalist, July 16, 2019, https://thefederalist.com/2019/07/16/3-reasons-joe-bidens-health-care-plan-merely-socialism-lite/.

3.   Ibid.

4.   Sally Pipes, "Bidencare Is Bad News," InsideSources, September 3, 2019, https://www.insidesources.com/bidencare-is-bad-news/.

5.   Ibid.

6.   "Healthcare," Joe Biden's campaign website, https://joebiden.com/healthcare/.

7.   Jon Walker, "Biden Wants to Expand the ACA. Blue States Can't Figure Out How to Run It in the First Place," The Intercept, March 6, 2020, https://theintercept.com/2020/03/06/biden-campaign-health-care-platform-affordable-care-act/.

8.   Reid J. Epstein and Abby Goodnough, "Joe Biden, Echoing Obama, Pledges to Shore Up the Affordable Care Act," *New York Times*, July 15, 2019, https://www.nytimes.com/2019/07/15/us/politics/biden-health-care.html.

Chapter 8: Biden Will Crush Religious Freedom

1.   "Joe Biden for the LGBTQ+ Community," Joe Biden's campaign website, https://joebiden.com/lgbtq/.

2.   Dan Casey, "Cut the 10 Commandments Down to 6?" *Roanoke Times*, May 7, 2012, https://www.roanoke.com/news/local/cut-the-10-commandments-down-to-6/article_9109b1b5-a967-52e3-9c38-6ef5012c453c.html.

3.   "New Gay Army," *Washington Times*, September 26, 2010, https://www.washingtontimes.com/news/2010/sep/16/new-gay-army/.

4.   Mairead McArdle, "Biden: 'There Is No Room for Compromise' on Transgender Rights," *National Review*, January 27, 2020, https://www.nationalreview.com/news/biden-there-is-no-room-for-compromise-on-transgender-rights/.

5. "Biden: We Believe in Freedom of Religion, That's Why I'll End the Muslim Ban," Grabien, July 11, 2019, https://grabien.com/story.php?id=243173.

6. Max Fisher, "Conservatives Furious over NASA Muslim Outreach," *The Atlantic*, July 7, 2010, https://www.theatlantic.com/technology/archive/2010/07/conservatives-furious-over-nasa-muslim-outreach/344960/.

Chapter 9: Biden's Green New Deal

1. Zack Colman and Natasha Korecki, "Plagiarism Charge Hits Biden Climate Change Plan," *Politico*, June 4, 2019, https://www.politico.com/story/2019/06/04/plagiarism-biden-climate-change-plan-1504950.

2. "Climate: Joe's Plan for a Clean Energy Revolution and Environmental Justice," Joe Biden's campaign website, https://joebiden.com/climate/.

3. Ibid.

4. Alexandra Kelley, "Biden Tells Coal Miners to 'Learn to Code,'" *The Hill*, December 31, 2019, https://thehill.com/changing-america/enrichment/education/476391-biden-tells-coal-miners-to-learn-to-code.

5. "Climate: Joe's Plan for a Clean Energy Revolution," Joe Biden's campaign website, https://joebiden.com/climate/.

6. Ibid.

7. Ibid.

8. Ibid.

9. Mandy Gunasekara, "2020 Election: Joe Biden's Climate Change Revolution Plan Shows He's Not Moderate Material," *USA Today*, June 12, 2019, https://www.usatoday.com/story/opinion/2019/06/12/joe-biden-radical-green-new-deal-plan-moderate-column/1365919001/.

Chapter 10: Biden's Foreign Policy Follies and Corruption

1. Branko Marcetic, "Joe Biden Helped Pull the Democrats to the Right," *Jacobin*, February 20, 2020, https://www.jacobinmag.com/2020/02/yesterdays-man-case-against-joe-biden-new-deal-reagan.

2. "Joe Biden," Discover the Networks, https://www.discoverthenetworks.org/individuals/joe-biden/.

3. Joe Biden, "Why America Must Lead Again: Rescuing U.S. Foreign Policy after Trump," *Foreign Affairs*, March/April 2020, https://www.

foreignaffairs.com/articles/united-states/2020-01-23/
why-america-must-lead-again.

4. Ibid.

5. Glenn Kessler, "Biden's Claim That He Didn't Tell Obama Not to Launch bin Laden Raid," *Washington Post*, January 8, 2020, https://www.washingtonpost.com/politics/2020/01/08/bidens-claim-that-he-didnt-tell-obama-not-launch-bin-laden-raid/.

6. Evan Osnos, "The Evolution of Joe Biden," *New Yorker*, July 28, 2014, https://www.newyorker.com/magazine/2014/07/28/biden-agenda.

7. Zeke Miller, "Biden: I 'Reject' Dick Cheney's Stance on Defense Spending," *Time*, July 16, 2014, https://time.com/2993511/biden-cheney/.

8. John MacDonald, "Joe Biden—Why Would Veterans Support Him?" *Lowell Sun*, April 15, 2020, https://www.lowellsun.com/2020/04/15/joe-biden-why-would-veterans-support-him/.

9. Herb Keinon, "How Would a Joe Biden Presidency Be for Israel?" *Jerusalem Post*, March 12, 2020, https://www.jpost.com/israel-news/how-would-a-joe-biden-presidency-be-for-israel-620801.

10. "Remarks by Vice President Biden," https://obamawhitehouse.archives.gov/the-press-office/2012/02/14/remarks-vice-president-biden-and-chinese-vice-president-xi-us-and-china-.

11. Tom Cotton, "Joe Biden Is China's Choice for President," *National Review*, March 11, 2020, https://www.nationalreview.com/2020/03/joe-biden-is-chinas-choice-for-president/.

12. Nels Frye, "Why China Is Rooting for Joe Biden to Win 2020 Presidential Race," *New York Post*, March 12, 2020, https://nypost.com/2020/03/12/why-china-is-rooting-for-joe-biden-to-win-2020-presidential-race/.

13. Alex Pareene, "Biden's Incoherent, China-Bashing Attack on Trump," *New Republic*, April 21, 2020, https://newrepublic.com/article/157393/bidens-incoherent-china-bashing-attack-trump.

14. Philip Bump, "Robert Gates Thinks Joe Biden Hasn't Stopped Being Wrong for 40 Years," *The Atlantic*, January 7, 2014, https://www.theatlantic.com/politics/archive/2014/01/robert-gates-thinks-joe-biden-hasnt-stopped-being-wrong-40-years/356785/.

Chapter 11: Biden: Champion of Failing Public Education

1. Matt Viser, "Joe Biden Wins the Endorsement of the National Education Association," *Washington Post*, March 14, 2020, https://www.washingtonpost.com/politics/joe-biden-wins-the-endorsement-of-the-national-education-association/2020/03/14/d53213ba-6637-11ea-b3fc-7841686c5c57_story.html.
2. "Education: Joe's Plan for Educators, Students, and Our Future," Joe Biden's campaign website, https://joebiden.com/education/.
3. Ibid.
4. Ibid.
5. Peter Hasson, "Joe Biden Touts Opposition to School Vouchers, despite Sending Sons to Posh Private School," Daily Caller, January 23, 2020, https://dailycaller.com/2020/01/23/joe-biden-vouchers-sons-private-school/.

Chapter 12: Biden's Identity Politics

1. Molly Nagle, "Joe Biden Gives Pitch on Uniting the Country in Philadelphia," ABC News, May 18, 2019, https://abc11.com/joe-biden-heads-to-philadelphia-to-give-pitch-on-uniting-the-country/5306659/.
2. "Joe Biden: We Have to End 'Divisive Partisan Politics,'" PBS, October 21, 2015, https://www.pbs.org/weta/washingtonweek/web-video/joe-biden-we-have-end-divisive-partisan-politics.
3. Eric Bradner and Maeve Reston, "Joe Biden Takes Trump Head-On over Charlottesville in Announcement Video," CNN, April 25, 2019, https://www.cnn.com/2019/04/25/politics/joe-biden-charlottesville-trump-2020-launch/index.html.
4. Emily Larsen, "Biden Falsely Says Trump Has 'Yet Once to Condemn White Supremacy,'" *Washington Examiner*, February 9, 2020, https://www.washingtonexaminer.com/news/biden-falsely-says-trump-has-yet-once-to-condemn-white-supremacy.
5. Robert Farley, "Trump Has Condemned White Supremacists," factcheck.org, February 11, 2020, https://www.factcheck.org/2020/02/trump-has-condemned-white-supremacists/.
6. Rodney Hawkins, "Biden Tells African-American Audience GOP Ticket Would Put Them 'Back in Chains,'" CBS, August 14, 2012, https://www.cbsnews.com/news/

biden-tells-african-american-audience-gop-ticket-would-put-them-back-in-chains/.

7. Zak Cheney-Rice, "Joe Biden Forgets What the Racists He Worked with Were Wearing," *New York*, January 22, 2020, https://nymag.com/intelligencer/2020/01/joe-biden-martin-luther-king-jr-day-remarks.html.

8. Matt Ford, "Biden's Diversity Promises Are Identity Politics at Their Best," *New Republic*, March 16, 2020, https://newrepublic.com/article/156945/bidens-diversity-promises-identity-politics-best.

9. Wilson Wong, "Biden Says He'd Pick Michelle Obama as a Running Mate 'in a Heartbeat,'" NBC, April 27, 2020, https://www.nbcnews.com/politics/elections/biden-says-he-d-pick-michelle-obama-vice-president-heartbeat-n1192071.

10. Sarah Mucha, "Biden Says Vice Presidential Committee 'Looking at More than a Dozen Women,'" Fox 5 Vegas News, May 2, 2020, https://www.fox5vegas.com/news/us_world_news/biden-says-vice-presidential-committee-looking-at-more-than-a-dozen-women/article_0e07f429-a634-5f8d-b565-2650f7678856.amp.html.

11. Jonathan Turley, "Did Biden Realize His Discriminatory Pledge for His Supreme Court Pick?" *The Hill*, March 17, 2020, https://thehill.com/opinion/judiciary/487961-did-biden-realize-his-discriminatory-pledge-for-his-supreme-court-pick.

12. Eric Levitz, "Will Black Voters Still Love Biden When They Remember Who He Was?" *New York*, March 12, 2019, https://nymag.com/intelligencer/2019/03/joe-biden-record-on-busing-incarceration-racial-justice-democratic-primary-2020-explained.html.

13. Jamelle Bouie, "The Trouble with Biden," *New York Times*, March 11, 2019, https://www.nytimes.com/2019/03/11/opinion/biden-busing-integration.html.

14. Branko Marcetic, "The Making of Joe Biden's Conservative Democratic Politics," *Jacobin*, February 22, 2020, https://www.jacobinmag.com/2020/02/yesterdays-man-case-against-joe-biden-busing.

15. Alison Durkee, "Anita Hill Eviscerates Joe Biden's 'Apology' in Scathing Interview," *Vanity Fair*, April 25, 2019, https://www.vanityfair.com/news/2019/04/anita-hill-eviscerates-bidens-apology-in-scathing-interview.

16. Li Zhou, "The Joe Biden and Anita Hill Controversy, Explained," Vox, April 29, 2019, https://www.vox.com/

policy-and-politics/2019/3/27/18262482/
joe-biden-anita-hill-2020-christine-blasey-ford-brett-kavanaugh.

17. Pratik Chougule, "Barack Obama: The Great Divider," *National Interest*, December 31, 2016, https://nationalinterest.org/feature/ barack-obama-the-great-divider-17791.

18. Jessica Chasmar, "Joe Biden: 'Dregs of Society' Support Donald Trump," *Washington Times*, September 17, 2018, https://www.washingtontimes. com/news/2018/sep/17/joe-biden-dregs-society-have-ally-donald-trump/.

Chapter 13: Creepy Joe

1. Steven Nelson, "Biden Swims Naked, Upsetting Female Secret Service Agents, Book Claims," U.S. News & World Report, August 1, 2014, https://www.usnews.com/news/blogs/washington-whispers/2014/08/01/ biden-swims-naked-upsetting-female-secret-service-agents-book-claims.

2. Lucy Flores, "An Awkward Kiss Changed How I Saw Joe Biden," The Cut, March 29, 2019, https://www.thecut.com/2019/03/an-awkward-kiss-changed-how-i-saw-joe-biden.html.

3. Neil Vigdor, "Connecticut Woman Says Then–Vice President Joe Biden Touched Her Inappropriately at a Greenwich Fundraiser in 2009," *Hartford Courant*, April 1, 2019, https://www.courant.com/politics/ hc-pol-biden-grabbed-aide-20190401-vl7chim3hrdjtcwu2tszrhozzm-story.html.

4. Mollie Hemingway, "Holy Hell Would Be Unleashed on 'Handsy' Joe Biden If He Were Conservative," The Federalist, January 7, 2015, https:// thefederalist.com/2015/01/07/ holy-hell-would-be-unleashed-on-handsy-joe-biden-if-he-were-conservative/.

5. Liza Featherstone, "For Elite Democrats, Joe Biden's Candidacy Means Ditching #MeToo," *Jacobin*, March 30, 2020, https://jacobinmag. com/2020/03/tara-reade-joe-biden-me-too-bernie-sanders-feminism.

6. Britni de la Cretaz, "Joe Biden Faces Sexual Assault Allegations from a Former Staffer," Yahoo News, March 26, 2020, https://news.yahoo. com/joe-biden-faces-sexual-assault-181441242.html.

7. Natasha Korecki, "Court Filing Shows Reade Spoke of Harassment in Biden's Office," *Politico*, May 8, 2020, https://www.politico.com/ news/2020/05/08/ court-filing-shows-reade-spoke-of-harassment-in-bidens-office-245718.

8. Rich McHugh, "A Former Neighbor of Joe Biden's Accuser Tara Reade Has Come Forward to Corroborate Her Sexual-Assault Account, Saying Reade Discussed the Allegations in Detail in the Mid-1990s," Business Insider, April 27, 2020, https://www.businessinsider.com/former-neighbor-corroborates-joe-bidens-accuser-2020-4.

9. Philip Rucker, "Joe Biden: When a Woman Alleges Sexual Assault, Presume She Is Telling the Truth," *Washington Post*, September 17, 2018, https://www.washingtonpost.com/politics/joe-biden-when-a-woman-alleges-sexual-assault-presume-she-is-telling-the-truth/2018/09/17/7718c532-badd-11e8-a8aa-860695e7f3fc_story.html.

10. Tucker Carlson, "Feminist Movement Is Fake, Only Cares about Power. That's Why Gillibrand Is Friends with Biden," Fox News, April 30, 2020, https://www.foxnews.com/opinion/tucker-carlson-feminist-movement-is-fake-only-cares-about-power-thats-why-gillibrand-is-friends-with-biden.

11. Katie Halper, "Tara Reade Says Joe Biden Sexually Assaulted Her. She Deserves to Be Heard," *The Guardian*, April 24, 2020, https://www.theguardian.com/commentisfree/2020/apr/24/joe-biden-sexual-assault-claim-tara-reade-deserves-to-be-heard-katie-halper.

12. "The Biden Plan to End Violence against Women," Joe Biden's campaign website, https://joebiden.com/vawa/.

13. Eli Watkins and Kevin Bohn, "Biden Responds to Lucy Flores' Allegation, Says 'Not Once' Does He Believe He Acted Inappropriately," CNN, April 1, 2019, https://www.cnn.com/2019/03/31/politics/joe-biden-lucy-flores/index.html.

14. Linda Hirshman, "I Believe Tara Reade. I'm Voting for Joe Biden Anyway," *New York Times*, May 6, 2020, https://www.nytimes.com/2020/05/06/opinion/tara-reade-joe-biden-vote.html.

15. Byron York, "Joe Biden in 2000: No Man Has the Right to Touch a Woman without Her Consent," *Washington Examiner*, February 18, 2015, https://www.washingtonexaminer.com/joe-biden-in-2000-no-man-has-the-right-to-touch-a-woman-without-her-consent.

Chapter 14: Serial Plagiarist

1. Charlie Bradley, "Joe Biden Shock: How Trump's Rival Plagiarised a Neil Kinnock Speech in Campaign Disaster," *Express*, December 3,

2019, https://www.express.co.uk/news/world/1212589/
joe-biden-news-trump-plagiarised-neil-kinnock-us-election-2020-spt.

2. Maureen Dowd, "Biden's Debate Finale: An Echo from Abroad," *New
    York Times*, September 12, 1987, https://www.nytimes.com/1987/09/12/
    us/biden-s-debate-finale-an-echo-from-abroad.html.

3. Paul Taylor, "Biden Admits Plagiarizing in Law School," *Washington
    Post*, September 18, 1987, https://www.washingtonpost.com/archive/
    politics/1987/09/18/
    biden-admits-plagiarizing-in-law-school/53047c90-c16d-4f3a-9317-
    a106be8f6102/.

4. Ibid.

5. R. W. Apple Jr., "Biden's Waterloo? Too Soon to Tell," *New York Times*,
    September 18, 1987, https://www.nytimes.com/1987/09/18/us/biden-s-
    waterloo-too-soon-to-tell.html.

6. Amy Sherman, "Joe Biden Stated on February 11, 2020 in a Campaign
    Event in South Carolina: 'I Had the Great Honor of Being Arrested with
    Our U.N. Ambassador on the Streets of Soweto Trying to Get to See
    (Nelson Mandela) on Robbens Island," Politifact, March 4, 2020,
    https://www.politifact.com/factchecks/2020/mar/04/joe-biden/
    joe-bidens-pants-fire-claim-about-his-arrest-south/.

7. Carl Hamilton, "Daughter of Man in '72 Biden Crash Seeks Apology
    from Widowed Senator," *Newark Post*, October 30, 2008, https://www.
    newarkpostonline.com/news/local/daughter-of-man-in-72-biden-crash-
    seeks-apology-from-widowed-senator/article_6c9a477e-63be-561b-
    b771-1330b4cda02d.html.

Chapter 15: Obama's Blundering Veep

1. Jimmy Orr, "Biden Does Not Derail Agreement on Stimulus Bill,"
    Christian Science Monitor, February 6, 2009, https://www.csmonitor.
    com/USA/Politics/The-Vote/2009/0206/
    biden-does-not-derail-agreement-on-stimulus-bill.

2. Evan Osnos, "The Evolution of Joe Biden," *New Yorker*, July 20, 2014,
    https://www.newyorker.com/magazine/2014/07/28/biden-agenda.

3. Ibid.

4. Claire Suddath, "Obama's Middle-Class Task Force Has No Middle
    Class," *Time*, March 4, 2009, http://content.time.com/time/politics/
    article/0,8599,1882913,00.html.

5. Andrew Cockburn, "No Joe!" *Harper's Magazine*, March 2019, https://harpers.org/archive/2019/03/joe-biden-record/.

6. Alan Cosgrove, "Joe Biden Holds Record for Being Wrong the Most Times on Foreign Policy," Fantasy Politics USA, April 28, 2012, https://fantasypoliticsusa.com/joe-biden-holds-record-for-being-wrong-the-most-times-in-foreign-policy/.

7. Jonathan Martin, "Book Details Obama Aides' Talks about Replacing Joe Biden on 2012 Ticket," *New York Times*, October 31, 2013, https://www.nytimes.com/2013/11/01/us/politics/book-details-consideration-of-replacing-biden-on-2012-ticket.html.

8. David Harsanyi, "Liberals Keep Mispresenting the 'Biden Rule,'" *National Review*, February 13, 2020, https://www.nationalreview.com/corner/liberals-keep-misrepresenting-the-biden-rule/.

9. Siraj Hashmi, "Lies and Scandals: What Joe Biden Conveniently Forgets from Obama's Eight Years," *Washington Examiner*, June 17, 2019, https://www.washingtonexaminer.com/opinion/lies-and-scandals-what-joe-biden-conveniently-forgets-from-obamas-eight-years.

10. Hunter DeRensis, "Why Hasn't Barack Obama Endorsed Joe Biden for President Yet?" *National Interest*, March 2, 2020, https://nationalinterest.org/blog/buzz/why-hasnt-barack-obama-endorsed-joe-biden-president-yet-129017.

Chapter 16: The Biden Family Business: Corruption

1. Peter Schweizer, *Profiles in Corruption: Abuse of Power by America's Progressive Elite* (New York: HarperCollins, 2020), 48.

2. Ibid., 54.

3. Ibid., 61.

4. Ibid., 73.

5. Ibid., 84.

6. Ibid., 91.

7. Branko Marcetic, "Joe Biden Is a Disaster Waiting to Happen," *Jacobin*, April 25, 2019, https://www.jacobinmag.com/2019/04/joe-biden-2020-presidential-campaign-record.

8. Ben Schreckinger, "Biden Inc.," *Politico*, August 2, 2019, https://www.politico.com/magazine/story/2019/08/02/

joe-biden-investigation-hunter-brother-hedge-fund-money-2020-campaign-227407.

9.   Emily Larsen, "'Middle-Class Joe' Cozied Up to Credit Card Companies and Made Filing for Bankruptcy Harder," *Washington Examiner*, April 18, 2019, https://www.washingtonexaminer.com/news/middle-class-joe-cozied-up-to-credit-card-companies-and-made-filing-for-bankruptcy-harder.

10. Byron York, "The Senator From MBNA," *American Spectator*, January 1998, https://spectator.org/63981_senator-mbna-our-january-1998-issue/.

11. Larsen, "'Middle-Class Joe.'"

12. Tim Murphy, "House of Cards," *Mother Jones*, November/December 2019, https://www.motherjones.com/politics/2019/11/biden-bankruptcy-president/.

13. Arthur Delaney, "Who Calls Joe Biden 'Middle-Class Joe'? Joe Biden Does, That's Who," HuffPost, March 6, 2019, https://www.huffingtonpost.ca/entry/joe-biden-middle-class_n_5c8032d8e4b06ff26ba55799?ri18n=true.

14. Zephyr Teachout, "'Middle Class' Joe Biden Has a Corruption Problem—It Makes Him a Weak Candidate," *The Guardian*, January 20, 2020, https://www.theguardian.com/commentisfree/2020/jan/20/joe-biden-corruption-donald-trump.

15. Taylor Borden, "Joe Biden Is Now the Clear Democratic Front-Runner. Here's How the Former VP Went from 'Middle-Class Joe' to Millionaire—and Built a $9 million Fortune along the Way," Business Insider, March 11, 2020, https://www.businessinsider.com/joe-biden-net-worth-lifestyle-real-estate-family-wealth-assets-2020-1.

16. York, "The Senator From MBNA."

17. Edward-Isaac Dovere, "The Sanders and Biden Families Have Been Cashing in for Years," *The Atlantic*, March 2, 2020, https://www.theatlantic.com/politics/archive/2020/03/bernie-sanders-joe-biden-enriched-their-families/607159/.

18. Sarah Kleiner, "9 Things to Know about Joe Biden," Center for Public Integrity, April 25, 2019, https://publicintegrity.org/politics/elections/presidential-profiles-2020/joe-biden/.

19. Ryan Grim, "Joe Biden's Family Has Been Cashing in on His Career for Decades. Democrats Need to Acknowledge That," The Intercept, October 9, 2019, https://theintercept.com/2019/10/09/joe-hunter-biden-family-money/.

20. Patrick Howley, "EXCLUSIVE: Hunter Biden Ashley Madison Account Created at College He Taught At," Breitbart, August 27, 2015, https://www.breitbart.com/politics/2015/08/27/exclusive-hunter-biden-ashley-madison-account-created-at-college-he-taught-at/.

21. Grim, "Joe Biden's Family Has Been Cashing in on His Career for Decades."

22. Adam Entous, "Will Hunter Biden Jeopardize His Father's Campaign?" *New Yorker*, July 1, 2019, https://www.newyorker.com/magazine/2019/07/08/will-hunter-biden-jeopardize-his-fathers-campaign.

23. Nadine Shubailat, "Exclusive: Hunter Biden Talks Getting Married after 6 Days and Why His Life Is in 'the Best Place I've Ever Been,'" ABC News, October 17, 2019, https://abcnews.go.com/Politics/exclusive-hunter-biden-talks-married-days-life-best/story?id=66333924.

24. Ibid.

25. John Solomon, "Joe Biden's 2020 Ukrainian Nightmare: A Closed Probe Is Revived," *The Hill*, April 1, 2019, https://thehill.com/opinion/white-house/436816-joe-bidens-2020-ukrainian-nightmare-a-closed-probe-is-revived.

26. "The Biden Plan to Guarantee Government Works for the People," Joe Biden's campaign website, https://joebiden.com/governmentreform/.

Chapter 17: Counterfeit Catholicism

1. Bill Schneider, "The Role of Catholic Voters," CNN, April 8, 2005, https://www.cnn.com/2005/POLITICS/04/08/catholic.voters/index.html.

2. Jessica Martinez and Gregory A. Smith, "How the Faithful Voted: A Preliminary 2016 Analysis," Pew Research Center, November 9, 2016, https://www.pewresearch.org/fact-tank/2016/11/09/how-the-faithful-voted-a-preliminary-2016-analysis/.

3. Matt Malone, "'Everyone's Entitled to Dignity': A Conversation with Joseph R. Biden Jr.," *America*, September 29, 2015, https://www.americamagazine.org/issue/everyones-entitled-dignity.

4. Ben Smith, "Differing on Stem Cells," *Politico*, September 9, 2008, https://www.politico.com/blogs/ben-smith/2008/09/differing-on-stem-cells-011670.

5. Eric Bradner, "Joe Biden Was Denied Communion at Catholic Church in South Carolina," CNN, October 29, 2019, https://www.cnn.com/2019/10/29/politics/joe-biden-denied-communion-south-carolina-catholic-church/index.html.

6. Ibid.

7. Glenn Thrush, "Communion for Biden," *Politico*, November 11, 2008, https://www.politico.com/blogs/ben-smith/2008/11/communion-for-biden-014134.

8. Magan Crane, "'He Went to the Press about It.' Biden on the Priest Who Denied Him Communion," PBS, November 1, 2019, https://www.pbs.org/newshour/politics/he-went-to-the-press-about-it-biden-on-the-priest-who-denied-him-communion.

9. Ibid.

10. Paul Kane, "Politicians Thought They Knew the Cardinal among Them. They Didn't," *Washington Post*, August 2, 2018, https://www.washingtonpost.com/powerpost/politicians-thought-they-knew-the-cardinal-among-them—they-didnt/2018/08/01/2078ae44-94ff-11e8-810c-5fa705927d54_story.html.

11. Hanna Trudo, "Biden: Pope Francis Wouldn't Endorse Sanders' Policies," *Politico*, April 15, 2016, https://www.politico.com/story/2016/04/joe-biden-pope-bernie-sanders-222040.

12. Mark Woods, "Jeb Bush Blames Pope Francis for Rise of Trump," *Christianity Today*, July 12, 2016, https://www.christiantoday.com/article/jeb-bush-blames-pope-francis-for-rise-of-trump/90389.htm.

13. "Highlights from Joe Biden's Vision for America," Joe Biden's campaign website, https://joebiden.com/catholics/.

Chapter 18: The Flip-Flopper

1. Brittany Hunter, "Joe Biden: The Architect of America's Disastrous War on Drugs," Foundation for Economic Education, April 25, 2019, https://fee.org/articles/joe-biden-the-architect-of-america-s-disastrous-war-on-drugs/.

2. Tom Angell, "Joe Biden Is Frustrated People Think He Still Believes Marijuana Is a Gateway Drug," *Forbes*, March 6, 2020, https://www.forbes.com/sites/tomangell/2020/03/06/joe-biden-is-frustrated-people-think-he-still-believes-marijuana-is-a-gateway-drug/#4ff507f09aa2.

3. Ibid.

4. "Joe Biden on Drugs," On the Issues, https://www.ontheissues.org/2020/
    Joe_Biden_Drugs.htm.

5. Chris Cillizza, "Why Joe Biden's Flip-Flop on the Hyde Amendment
    Matters," CNN, June 7, 2019, https://www.cnn.com/2019/06/07/
    politics/joe-biden-hyde-amendment-2020/index.html.

6. Richard Cohen, "Joe Biden Reeks of Insincerity," *Washington Post*, June
    10, 2019, https://www.washingtonpost.com/opinions/joe-biden-reeks-of-
    insincerity/2019/06/10/1086086a-8bb2-11e9-8f69-a2795fca3343_story.
    html.

7. Eddie Scarry, "Joe Biden Reverses His Position on Government
    Healthcare for Illegal Immigrants," *Washington Examiner*, July 5, 2019,
    https://www.washingtonexaminer.com/opinion/
    joe-biden-reverses-his-position-on-government-healthcare-for-illegal-
    immigrants.

8. "The Biden Plan for Bankruptcy Reform," Joe Biden's campaign website,
    https://joebiden.com/bankruptcyreform/.

9. Matthew Yglesias, "Joe Biden's Effort to Heal the Breach with Elizabeth
    Warren on Bankruptcy, Explained," Vox, March 16, 2020, https://www.
    vox.com/2020/3/16/21181500/joe-biden-elizabeth-warren-bankruptcy.

10. Bryan Anderson, "Joe Biden on Housing: 'No One Should Pay More
    Than 30 Percent of Their Income," *Sacramento Bee*, January 14, 2020,
    https://www.sacbee.com/news/politics-government/capitol-alert/
    article239254133.html.

11. "The Joe Biden Plan for Investing in Our Communities through
    Housing," Joe Biden's campaign website, https://joebiden.com/housing/.

12. Ibid.

13. Ibid.

14. Ibid.

Chapter 19: The Campaign Ahead

1. Eliza Relman, "Joe Biden Suffers Blistering Loss in New Hampshire,
    with the Former Frontrunner Winning No Delegates Just a Week after a
    Disastrous Iowa Caucus Showing," Business Insider, February 11, 2020,
    https://www.businessinsider.com/
    joe-biden-suffers-huge-2020-loss-in-new-hampshire-primary-2020-2.

2. Jane C. Timm and Dareh Gregorian, "Clyburn Calls for Democrats to
    'Shut This Primary Down' If Biden Has Big Night," NBC, March 10,

2020, https://www.nbcnews.com/politics/2020-election/clyburn-calls-democrats-shut-primary-down-if-biden-has-big-n1155131.

3. Ryan Grim, "'The Waters Parted for Biden,'" The Intercept, March 10, 2020, https://theintercept.com/2020/03/10/bernie-sanders-joe-biden-michigan/.

4. Mark Moore, "Joe Biden Promises to Put Beto O'Rourke in Charge of Gun Control," *New York Post*, March 3, 2020, https://nypost.com/2020/03/03/joe-biden-promises-to-put-beto-orourke-in-charge-of-gun-control/.

5. Ben Mathis-Lilley, "Joe Biden Has Cured Democrats of Their Belief in a Savior President," Slate, March 11, 2020, https://slate.com/news-and-politics/2020/03/joe-biden-has-cured-democrats-of-their-belief-in-a-savior-president.html.

6. Eric Bradner and Sarah Mucha, "Biden Says He's a 'Bridge' to New 'Generation of Leaders' while Campaigning with Harris, Booker, Whitmer," CNN, March 9, 2020, https://www.cnn.com/2020/03/09/politics/joe-biden-bridge-new-generation-of-leaders/index.html.

7. Jeff Jacoby, "'Moderate' Joe Biden Has Moved Way to the Left," *Boston Globe*, March 11, 2020, https://www.bostonglobe.com/2020/03/11/opinion/moderate-joe-biden-has-moved-way-to-left/.

8. Katie Glueck, Shane Goldmacher, and Glenn Thrush, "Now Comes the Hard Part for Joe Biden," *New York Times*, April 8, 2020, https://www.nytimes.com/2020/04/08/us/politics/biden-sanders-campaign-policy.html.

9. Laura Barron-Lopez and Holly Otterbein, "Biden Mounts Behind-the-Scenes Mission to Win Over Wary Progressives," *Politico*, March 28, 2020, https://www.politico.com/news/2020/03/28/joe-biden-plan-to-court-young-progressives-151787.

10. Adam Serwer, "Fear of a Counterrevolution," *The Atlantic*, March 17, 2020, https://www.theatlantic.com/ideas/archive/2020/03/the-democrats-big-gamble-on-joe-biden/608128/.

11. Katie Glueck and Jonathan Martin, "Joe Biden Shakes Up Campaign Leadership, Elevating Anita Dunn," *New York Times*, February 7, 2020, https://www.nytimes.com/2020/02/07/us/politics/joe-biden-anita-dunn.html.

12. "#YouthVote Letter to Joe Biden," NextGen America, https://nextgenamerica.org/Biden-letter/.

13. Tal Axelrod, "Biden Says His Administration Could Help Grow 'Bench' for Democrats," *The Hill*, April 4, 2020, https://thehill.com/homenews/

campaign/491147-biden-says-his-administration-could-help-grow-bench-for-democrats.

14. Lloyd Green, "Where There's Trouble, You'll Usually Find Joe Biden," *The Daily Beast*, April 14, 2017, https://www.thedailybeast.com/where-theres-trouble-youll-usually-find-joe-biden.

15. Ryan Lizza, "Why Biden's Retro Inner Circle Is Succeeding So Far," *Politico*, December 19, 2019, https://www.politico.com/news/magazine/2019/12/19/biden-2020-campaign-president-advisers-087410.

16. Sonam Sheth, "Here's Who Joe Biden Is Reportedly Considering for Top Positions in His Administration as He Touts a 'Return to Normal' Plan," Business Insider, March 9, 2020, https://www.businessinsider.com/who-joe-biden-will-appoint-to-top-cabinet-positions-axios-2020-3.

17. Katie Glueck, "Biden Steps Up Warnings of Possible Trump Disruption of Election," *New York Times*, April 24, 2020, https://www.nytimes.com/2020/04/24/us/politics/joseph-biden-trump-election.html.

Chapter 20: Should the Next President of the United States Be Senile, Scandal-Plagued, and Racially Offensive?

1. Steven Nelson, "Trump: They'll Put Joe Biden in 'a Home' If Elected President," *New York Post*, March 2, 2020, https://nypost.com/2020/03/02/trump-theyll-put-joe-biden-in-a-home-if-elected-president/.

2. Nick Corasaniti and Maggie Haberman, "'Geriatric,' 'China's Puppet': Trump Campaign Unleashes Ads Attacking Biden," *New York Times*, May 15, 2020, https://www.nytimes.com/2020/05/15/us/politics/trump-ads-joe-biden.html.

3. Glenn Greenwald, "Democrats and Their Media Allies Impugned Biden's Cognitive Fitness. Now They Feign Outrage," The Intercept, March 9, 2020, https://theintercept.com/2020/03/09/it-was-democrats-and-their-media-allies-who-impugned-bidens-cognitive-fitness-yet-now-feign-outrage/.

4. Ibid.

5. Ibid.

6. Ibid.

7. Brooke Singman, "Biden Says He Was 'Aware' of Michael Flynn Probe during Transition," Fox News, May 12, 2020, https://www.foxnews.com/politics/biden-says-he-was-aware-investigation-of-michael-flynn.

8. Jack Brewster, "Biden among Those Who Requested 'Unmasking' of Michael Flynn," *Forbes*, May 13, 2020, https://www.forbes.com/sites/jackbrewster/2020/05/13/biden-among-those-who-requested-unmasking-of-michael-flynn/#5331e4382a38.

9. "Joe Biden Says Voters 'Ain't Black' If They Support Trump," CNN, May 22, 2020, https://www.cnn.com/videos/politics/2020/05/22/joe-biden-you-aint-black-breakfast-club-mh-orig.cnn.

10. Scott Wong, "Clyburn Cringed at Biden's 'You Ain't Black' Remarks," *The Hill*, May 26, 2020, https://thehill.com/homenews/house/499520-clyburn-cringed-at-bidens-you-aint-black-remarks.

11. Ibid.

12. "Top 10 Joe Biden Gaffes," *Time*, no date, http://content.time.com/time/specials/packages/article/0,28804,1895156_1894977_1644536,00.html.

Appendix: No Longer Ready for Prime Time: Selected Recent Quotations from the Presumptive Democratic Nominee for President of the United States

1. Dominick Mastrangelo, "'You Know, the Thing': Biden Botches Declaration of Independence Quote during Campaign Stop," *Washington Examiner*, March 2, 2020, https://www.washingtonexaminer.com/news/you-know-the-thing-biden-botches-declaration-of-independence-quote-during-campaign-stop.

2. Johnathan Jones, "Biden Claims Twice That 'No Matter What' the COVID Cure Will Make Things Worse," Western Journal, March 24, 2020, https://www.westernjournal.com/biden-claims-twice-no-matter-covid-cure-will-make-things-worse/.

3. Anna North, "Biden's 'Lying Dog-Faced Pony Soldier' Moment Explained," Vox, February 10, 2020, https://www.vox.com/2020/2/10/21131327/biden-dog-faced-pony-soldier-new-hampshire.

4. Madlin Mekelburg, "Video Doesn't Show Biden Promising to 'Take Away Americans' Guns," Politifact, March 4, 2020, https://www.politifact.com/factchecks/2020/mar/13/conservative-daily/joe-biden-not-adopting-beto-orourkes-mandatory-buy/.

5.   Nicholas Wu, "Joe Biden, in Testy Interview, Says 'You Ain't Black' If You're Undecided between Him and Trump," *USA Today*, May 22, 2020, https://www.postcrescent.com/story/news/politics/elections/2020/05/22/biden-you-aint-black-if-you-cant-decide-between-trump-and-biden/5242706002/.

6.   Bo Erickson, "Joe Biden, Accused of Wanting to End 2nd Amendment, Responds: 'You're Full of Sh**,'" CBS News, March 10, 2020, https://www.cbsnews.com/news/biden-accused-of-wanting-to-end-2nd-amendment-responds-youre-full-of-shit/.

7.   HSTX Power, "The Last Word with Lawrence O'Donnell [Full] 3/9/20 MSNBC News Trump," YouTube, March 9, 2020, https://www.youtube.com/watch?v=HpZmCnNB424.

8.   Andrew Mark Miller, "'I Don't Know': Biden Appears to Lose Train of Thought while Reading Notes," *Washington Examiner*, June 11, 2020, https://www.washingtonexaminer.com/news/i-dont-know-biden-appears-to-lose-train-of-thought-while-reading-notes.

9.   Emily Larsen, "Biden Botches Criticism of Trump Tulsa Rally on Juneteenth as Other Democrats Say Timing Signals to 'White Supremacists,'" *Washington Examiner*, June 11, 2020, https://www.washingtonexaminer.com/news/biden-botches-criticism-of-trump-tulsa-rally-on-juneteeth-as-other-democrats-say-timing-signals-to-white-supremacists.

Index